CORONADO
and His Captains

by Camilla Campbell

ILLUSTRATIONS BY HARVE STEIN

Follett Publishing Company   CHICAGO

Library of Congress Catalog Card Number: 58-10090

To that eager explorer

DAN WILLIAM CAMPBELL

1

The
Secret
Journey

Young Francisco Vasquez de Coronado looked troubled as he came out of the viceroy's palace. He stopped to gaze for a moment at the great Plaza in front of him. The immense tree-shaded square, bright with flowers and filled with colorfully dressed people, always fascinated him. He saw it as the heart of Mexico City, his home for almost five years.

He was proud of the way the Spaniards had rebuilt the ancient Aztec city to their own taste in the twenty-odd years since Hernan Cortéz had conquered it. From where he stood he could see the cathedral, the college, hospitals, and monasteries. He could see the severe stone front of his own house on the south side of the Plaza.

He turned toward it now, walking faster as he drew near. He was still frowning as he nodded to the Indian servant who opened the heavy carved door onto a patio filled with flowers and singing birds. But the frown disappeared when he held out his arms toward the little girl who ran to meet him.

Lifting her to his shoulder, he went on to find his wife, a laughing-eyed young woman who had been called the most beautiful girl in New Spain.

"What did the viceroy want of you?" Doña Beatrice asked quickly.

"You will not be happy," Francisco warned her. "He has made me governor of the province of New Galicia."

She smiled. "But Francisco! What an honor!"

"Yes," he said, "but I must go alone. It is too far and too wild for you and Isabel."

Beatrice's smile faded. "Then why has he done this? I thought he was our friend!"

"He is sending scouts on a secret journey into the northern mountains. He wants me to get them ready and send them on their way."

Beatrice sighed but did not argue. Both she and Francisco knew that as a Spanish grandee he must do what his king, or his king's viceroy, wished him to do.

Francisco had been born in 1510 in Salamanca, Spain, into a family of lesser nobles. Ever since he had been old enough to know anything, he had known he would have to make his own way in the world, for he was a younger son in days when only the eldest inherited the family estates. For that reason, when he was twenty-five years old he had come to New Spain with the viceroy, Antonio de Mendoza. Within a year Mendoza had made him his personal secretary and had appointed him to the city council. And when Francisco had married Beatrice de Estrada, the viceroy had stood up with them in the church.

By March of 1539, young Governor Coronado was in Culiacan, the most northern village of the Spanish colony. In all New Spain, only the lands north of here were left unexplored, for no one had found a way through the mountain barrier.

Early one morning Francisco stood on the edge of the little town with the mayor, stocky gray-bearded Melchior Diaz. They were saying good-by to two men who, with only a small escort of friendly Indians, were to start the secret journey of exploration. One was Fray Marcos de Niza, a Franciscan missionary. He touched the silver cross swinging from his girdle and murmured, "*Señores*, I hope I shall not disappoint you and the vice-

7

roy." The gray-robed friar was no longer a young man.
He had already walked over a large part of the New
World, north and south. But he was eager to begin his
new adventure.

His guide was a tall black man named Estevan, a
Moorish slave, who knew of a pass through the mountains. He carried a feathered gourd rattle which he be-

lieved to be magic, for it had seen him safely through the wild lands once before. It had made the Indians think he was a great chieftain.

About ten years earlier, Estevan had been shipwrecked with Cabeza de Vaca and a party of Spaniards on the coast of what is now Texas. All of them had died except the Moor and three officers. After trying for six years, these four castaways had at last found their way to settlements in New Spain.

Because they had come down from the unknown north, shaggy-haired and dressed in animal skins, their adventure had filled the colony with wonder and with rumors. They brought news of strange kingdoms which they themselves had not seen but which they had been told about by the natives. Somewhere north of where they had traveled, there were walled towns of many-storied houses, inhabited by people wealthy in turquoises and emeralds. The rumors grew with each retelling until the men of New Spain believed that these towns had streets paved with gold.

The three weary officers had refused to go back as guides, but Estevan was willing.

"Who knows?" Melchior Diaz said. "We may be on the verge of the greatest discovery yet. Even another kingdom like the Aztecs'!"

Coronado turned to Fray Marcos. "You have learned the viceroy's instructions?"

The missionary rubbed his fringe of hair and grinned. "I wonder if there is anything His Excellency does not want to know about the land we seek! People, soil, climate, animals, minerals!"

Melchior Diaz added, "And rivers. And learn about the coast, especially whether some arm of the sea enters the land to make a good harbor. I am curious to know if this be part of Asia, as some men say."

"Aye, and if there be great mines of silver and gold, as other men say," the friar replied.

Coronado said earnestly, "Be sure to take possession of all the land in the name of God, King Charles, and Spain."

"Aye."

"Then go with God," Francisco murmured, and the men turned their faces northward and started forth.

In a few days an Indian runner brought back a report from Fray Marcos. All was going well; the natives were greeting them warmly. The young governor sent the report on to the viceroy in Mexico City, wishing he could carry it himself. But he must stay in New Galicia until the scouts returned.

Spring blossomed and gave way to summer, but

Coronado received no further word from Fray Marcos and Estevan. He busied himself learning all he could about this sprawling province he governed, and doing what he could to help its settlers.

One evening he rode in, hot and tired, to Compostela, the little red-dusted capital of New Galicia.

Fray Marcos was waiting for him! The friar was alone, his robe was tattered, his face haggard; but a light of glory burned in his dark eyes.

"I have found the best lands yet!" he assured the astonished governor in a fierce whisper. "But no one else must know until we can tell the viceroy."

Without taking time to eat or drink, Francisco sat on the edge of his chair and listened to the friar's story.

"The natives remembered Estevan and were friendly to us," he began. "At a village called Vacapa, we parted. The Moor was so eager I let him go ahead while I sent runners to the seacoast.

"Before he left me, we made a code. If he learned of a good land, he was to send back a cross as large as his hand. If the land was of great importance, the cross should be as large as two hands."

The friar caught his breath, then burst out, "Four days later I received from him a cross as tall as a man!"

"As tall as a man?" Coronado echoed, marveling.

"Yes! And a message that Estevan had news of the greatest kingdom in the world! It is called Cibola. Its houses are of stone, ten stories high. The very doors are lined with gold and studded with jewels. When I heard that, I rushed to catch up with the Moor, believe me! But fast as I went, I could not gain on him. How that man could walk! I took time only to claim the land for Spain, and hurried after him. I crossed wild rivers, valleys full of little towns, and deserted highlands, but still I did not overtake him. All along the way natives told me of the wonders of Cibola."

Francisco kept murmuring, "Yes, yes, go on." He forgot how weary he was, for he had to hear the end of the tale.

"Then I entered a wilderness which requires fifteen days to cross. On the other side is the city of Cibola. On the twelfth day in this long wilderness, an Indian who had been with Estevan stumbled back to me. He was sweating and breathless. The black man, he said, and all the natives with him, had been killed by the warriors of Cibola."

Coronado exclaimed, "Estevan—killed? What happened then?"

"The Indians with me were terrified. But I persuaded two of the chieftains to go with me to a hill. From its summit, Don Francisco, I looked upon the many-storied houses, their walls rising one upon the other and glittering in the sun as if made of gold, grander than the city of Mexico itself! I didn't tarry, but hurried back to bring word to you. With," he added ruefully, "more fear than food."

"As soon as you have rested," Francisco told him, "we will go to the viceroy together."

It was the end of summer. Francisco lay in his hammock, swinging himself gently with one foot, contented as a well-fed cat. Here he was, at last, back in his own flower-scented patio, listening to the murmur of the fountain and the busy little sounds from the kitchen. He could see Doña Beatrice arranging a bowl of yellow zinnias on the table of their favorite room. It had one side open to the patio and was full of songbirds in woven reed cages.

At his wife's summons, Coronado unwound himself from the hammock and joined her. An Indian serving girl set between them a meat pie steaming with spices. As Doña Beatrice reached for a black olive from a silver dish, she asked her husband, "What is the viceroy planning now, that he is so eager to see you this afternoon?"

Francisco shrugged. He didn't say so, but he had

a strong idea it had to do with Cibola. He had spent most of August helping Fray Marcos write the report of his journey for King Charles. They had given up trying to keep it secret, since the friar could not refrain from talking about it, even to his barber. By now there was hardly a man in the capital who wasn't plotting ways to find the golden kingdom. Only the viceroy's stern order that no one leave New Spain without his permission was holding them back.

The afternoon sun felt hot to Coronado as he came out of his cool house and walked toward the palace. All around him were flowers: growing, or for sale, or filling the little barges on the canal coming up from the floating gardens of Xochimilco.

And all around him was the sound of bells. All day they bonged or jingled, from morning *Ave Maria* to the *Angelus* at night. The flowers and bells and the throngs of Indians, peons, monks, and soldiers coming and going across the Plaza were all part of the spell which this old Aztec city cast over Francisco. If he had his way, he would never leave it.

He found the viceroy seated at the desk in his private room. Mendoza was a portly man with a look of calm dignity. Already people were calling him Mendoza the Good because of the sensible way he governed the colony. Now his dark brows were drawn together in thought. His pointed beard looked blacker against the white ruff of his velvet coat.

"I have decided to send an expedition to the new lands found by Fray Marcos," he said, "so that we may add the kingdom of Cibola to the Spanish empire."

Francisco nodded thoughtfully. "I have expected Your Grace to do that."

He was not sure he liked the way Mendoza looked at him then, with both question and humor in his eyes. "I shall send drummers into the Plaza tomorrow to beat for volunteers," the viceroy continued.

"In that case," Francisco replied, "let me be the first to offer my services." Then, because of that odd look still upon him, he added quickly, "Not to go on the expedition, you understand, but to help in its preparation."

He was more puzzled than ever when the viceroy threw back his head and laughed, even as he rose and put a hand on Francisco's shoulder. "You, my son, shall not only go on the expedition, you shall lead it. As my captain-general."

Francisco shuddered. This was even worse than being made governor of New Galicia! Thoughts tumbled through his head. It was bad enough to be away in New Galicia for months at a time. How much farther lay

Cibola? How long must one stay there? How long before he could come home again, to Doña Beatrice and their little daughter Isabel?

His words spilled out. "As you are my friend, Don Antonio, hear me! I say no, I will not do it!"

Mendoza answered gently. "I know you do not say that through fear of danger. You proved your courage when you put down that rebellion of slaves in the silver mines of the king." He went on softly, "There is not a man in New Spain, Don Francisco, who wouldn't give half his fortune to lead this army. Could I leave my post here, I would like nothing better than to explore Cibola myself."

Francisco tried once more. "Your Grace, I am not the man for this enterprise. I am no bold conqueror like Cortéz and Pizarro."

Mendoza grinned. "Which is all the better for the king and myself. We want this to be a peaceful conquest. You have calm judgment and an orderly mind. You have loyalty, and will receive loyalty from your men. Also, I know your sense of duty. You will accept."

Francisco could not decide if the last words were a question or an order, but it made no difference.

"I accept," he said slowly, and the two words changed his own life and the course of history.

2

Splendor
and
Death

There was an endless list of
things to be done, for Antonio de Mendoza wanted this
to be the best planned of
any exploration yet undertaken in the New World.

First a horseman went galloping through the jungles
and valleys to Culiacan with secret orders to Melchior
Diaz. The sturdy mayor was to take fifteen riders and
go north as Fray Marcos had gone. He was to find out
if the Indians along the trail were still friendly in spite
of the death of Estevan and his followers.

In Coronado's house, the table in the garden room
was no longer used for eating. It was piled high with
lists and bottles and boxes for Fray Marcos. Rested and

eager, the friar was ready to retrace his steps in order to act as guide and as a saver of heathen souls. For wherever in the New World the Spanish soldiers carried their swords, the Franciscans took their crosses. On this journey Fray Marcos would have with him four more long-robed missionaries. It was the pleasure of Doña Beatrice to help them gather together their oils and wines, their rosaries, crosses, and candles.

With the approval of the viceroy, Francisco drew up rules for the Mexican Indians who would go with him. They would not be slaves, but would be free to turn back whenever they wished. They were not to be burden-bearers as on some earlier expeditions. They would serve as scouts, horse wranglers, and herders.

As fast as he could buy cattle and sheep, Francisco set the Indians to trail-driving them to the grazing lands outside the village of Compostela, which was to be the starting point of the journey.

Mules were bought and laden with packs of trade goods. These hawk bells, red caps, Venetian glass beads, and colored cloths would be bartered for food along the way. Mendoza had ordered that nothing should be taken by force.

Because Fray Marcos had said that Cibola was not far from the sea, Mendoza arranged for two ships to stand by at the port of Acapulco on the Pacific coast. Into their holds went more bales of trade goods and large quantities of corn meal, beans, and wheat, and squawking chickens in cages. The ships were to start north when the expedition left, hugging the shoreline so that the men of the army could find them whenever they needed the supplies.

In the meantime, the captain-general was carrying out the most difficult task of all: the selection of his officers and men. News of the expedition had gone crackling through the colony like a forest fire, and volunteers of every kind had rushed to the capital. There were young grandees, leathery old soldiers, miners, farmers, ranchers, and clerks in such numbers that it was hard to keep the army small enough. To round out his forces, Francisco enlisted a mapmaker, an artist, several chroniclers, a surgeon, and a number of blacksmiths.

Before long the soft *clop clop* of hoofs was heard more and more often on the road to Compostela as Coronado sent his men on in small groups for the rendezvous there. They laughed and dreamed, planning deeds of daring and how to spend the fortunes they would find, and Francisco envied them their light hearts.

At the end of the year, there remained only the necessity of saying good-by to his family before he himself left for the rendezvous. This was even harder because of the small new daughter, Marina, who shared the nursery with Isabel.

Francisco put a finger under the tiny chin and looked into the baby's solemn dark eyes, knowing he would be a stranger to her when he returned. He gave Isabel a final hug; then he and Beatrice walked down the stairs hand in hand, across the patio, cold now in December, and to the carriage gate where his horse was waiting.

He turned in his saddle to look back at the warm smile and waving hand of his young wife. For the rest of the day he could still hear her last words to him, as he would remember them many and many a time on the trail: "God will go with you, Francisco. Good fortune will not desert you."

At last it was the twenty-second day of February, the end of planning and the beginning of action.

The day broke bright and clear, the rosy dawn echoing the red soil of Compostela. Francisco had been up an hour or more giving instructions to officers and grooms. Today everything must show perfection. The viceroy and his highest officials were here to review the cavalcade as it started on its quest.

At its head would ride a captain-general in gold.

When Coronado swung into his saddle, horse and man were a burnished shimmer of brushed chestnut coat, gold-fringed saddle blanket, and gilded armor—the gift of wealthy men of the colony who felt that nothing less would do for the seeker of golden cities. Coronado's slender figure was encased in golden armor, his tanned face topped with a golden helmet plumed with white. He touched a light spur to his horse and rode out to join the viceroy for inspection of his forces.

The silken banners were borne high by mounted men. Red, white, gold, black, they fluttered and popped in the dew-cooled breeze. Lance tips, breastplates, and bridles shot out splintered reflections of the early sun. Harness jingled as horses pulled against taut reins. The smell of clean horses, new leather, and crushed wet grass reached Coronado's nostrils pleasantly.

What hard-riding son of Spain could fail to be stirred by these sights and sounds? Francisco felt his spirits rise. There came over him a feeling of deep satisfaction, for here on the meadows of Compostela the long months of planning took on visible shape in this scene of splendor. He knew his work had been well done.

He looked at the viceroy, regal in crimson and black silk, mounted on a dancing black stallion, and saw on his face the same satisfaction. Francisco fervently hoped

that he would see the same expression there when he returned.

The two men rode together down the line of cavalry, which was formed into six companies. Most of the captains were Coronado's old and good friends. He and Mendoza took the salute of the two hundred mounted men. Then they passed the company of artillery, with its brass cannons mounted on cart wheels. They passed the infantry, over sixty buckskin-clad stalwarts standing at attention with lances and swords. Some carried the heavy guns called arquebuses.

Francisco noticed one man in the ranks whom he knew to be a Frenchman. Among the men who were going with the army to win new lands for Spain were, besides the Frenchman, five Portuguese, two Italians, and a Scot.

They passed the crowded forces of their thousand Indian allies, brave-looking in parrot-feather headdresses and armor of quilted cotton, and armed with bows and arrows, clubs, spears, slings, and javelins. Behind the Indians were the herds of horses, cattle, and sheep — more than fifteen hundred animals.

"Your food on the hoof," Mendoza said, smiling.

Francisco looked at the heavy-laden pack mules and replied, with a grin, "We can be glad that part of our food will carry itself."

By the time they had returned to the front of the line, a notary had finished taking down the name of every man, with the armor and weapons he carried and the number of his horses. Each man had furnished his own according to his ability. Those who were too poor had been equipped by Mendoza and other rich men with the expectation of being more than repaid out of the treasures of Cibola.

With a small escort the Franciscans had gone on several days' march ahead of the army. Only one remained, Fray Vittoria. Before him Francisco dismounted. He placed his right hand on the missal held by the friar and made his oath: "As a good Christian, vassal and servant of His Majesty, I shall cherish the service of God and His Majesty, obeying the commandments of the viceroy as a good gentleman and *hidalgo* should, with all my knowledge and understanding."

Then all the horsemen dismounted, and every man of the expedition repeated after the viceroy an oath of allegiance to their captain-general. After that they knelt on the grass while Fray Vittoria asked the blessing of God upon them and their journey.

The next morning, at bugle call, the companies reformed, and one of the most important explorations in all the Americas began.

Antonio de Mendoza, as if finding it hard to let the men go without him, swung up on his horse and led the way north with Coronado. The pounding rumble of hoofs grew louder behind them. On their left the Pacific Ocean was blue in the distance. The Sierra Madre lifted its purple peaks on the eastern horizon.

On the second day out, Francisco and the viceroy stopped on a rise and looked back. They could see their forces strung out for miles along the narrow trail.

The general shook his head. "It is a clumsy march. The men do not even know how to pack their saddlebags so they will stay on."

Mendoza chuckled. "They are learning, Don Francisco. They are learning fast or losing their possessions. And with such good cheer! Like boys on a holiday."

On that same day the viceroy left them to go back to the capital. Francisco told him, with a wry smile, "Would that we might change places, Your Grace."

Mendoza, shaking his head, replied, "Think of the glory which will be yours when you return."

As the days passed, Francisco presented to his men a picture of confidence and hope, keeping to himself the thoughts of how — should the expedition fail — the blame would be his, as surely as the glory if it succeeded. He was determined it should succeed.

The men stayed cheerful. They sang as they cut their way through jungles vivid with birds and flowers by day and eerie with the cries of wild animals at night. Even the marshes buzzing with mosquitoes did not still the laughter.

The rushing Rio Santiago delayed them several days.

It was too deep for the sheep to cross on foot, so the horse-men ferried them over in their arms, one at a time. The next four rivers they crossed were hard on the horses. Although shallow, they flowed through sandy lagoons which sucked at feet and hoofs.

When they reached the ruins of Chiametla, about halfway between Compostela and Culiacan, the general called a halt for rest.

"This was once a pleasant, pretty town," Lope de Samaniego told him sadly. "I know, because I was one of its founders."

Francisco looked at it now with raised eyebrows. The deserted houses and crumbled adobe walls gave it a ghostly air. Samaniego went on, "The Christians all left after Nuño de Guzman's cruelty to the natives made them hostile."

Francisco knew of Nuño de Guzman, once a governor of New Galicia. Three times he had tried, without success, to find the pass through the mountains toward which Fray Marcos was guiding them. Then Mendoza had sent him back to Spain in chains because of his harsh treatment of the Indians, many of whom he enslaved.

Lope de Samaniego, the army-master or second-in-command, was a veteran soldier well loved by the Spaniards. After pasturing the stock in the cleared places near the empty village, he took some men to look for corn in the abandoned fields.

"Do not get out of sight of one another," the general cautioned them. "There may be unfriendly heathens still about."

Before long he heard men running and shouting. From his tent he saw Captain Diego Lopez plunging through the press of curious soldiers. As the men quieted at sight of the captain's pale face and the burden he bore, Francisco went forward to meet him.

He stopped, shocked. The limp form in the captain's arms was the body of Lope de Samaniego, with the shaft of an arrow piercing the head!

As soon as Captain Lopez was relieved of his burden, he told the general what had happened. "While we were looking for corn, we heard a cry of distress and discovered that one of our soldiers was missing. We found him in some thickets, more frightened than hurt, although his arm had been cut by an arrow. He said some natives had tried to capture him. Since there was no sign of the Indians, Captain Samaniego raised his visor to look at the man's wounds. Out of nowhere, it seemed, a speeding, silent arrow found the opening of his headpiece. He died instantly."

Evening dropped peacefully over the ruins of Chiametla. But it brought no peace to the restless soldiers. They walked about from fire to fire, talking, discussing, arguing. Many thought the death of the veteran army-master an evil omen. Hadn't he been killed in the town he himself had helped to establish? Truly it was an evil thing, this first death among them, they said.

Francisco heard the mutterings. He knew, of course, that they were paying for the villainy of Nuño de Guzman, that they were the innocent victims of revenge meant for him. He knew, too, that the army-master's sudden death meant the end of the spirit of holiday for his soldiers.

Before he could move his army out of the crumbled village, Melchior Diaz and his squadron of horsemen came riding in from the north. Wind-whipped and ragged, they went straight to the general's tent. They had been gone four months and had ridden fifteen hundred miles, carrying out the viceroy's orders to retrace the trail of Fray Marcos.

3

To the
Red House
Ruins

Francisco took a long look at Melchior Diaz, sitting on a stool before him, his hands clapped to his knees. Twelve months ago, when they had stood together to send Fray Marcos and Estevan on their way, the mayor of Culiacan had been round of cheek and neatly barbered. Now he was lean-ribbed, his face was red and parched and his hair and beard matted. The general knew without words that his journey had been difficult.

"The natives are still friendly," Diaz assured Francisco. "But they have no food. The crops failed for lack of rain. We rode as far as a place called Red House, which lies at the beginning of the long wilderness Fray

Marcos told about. We were stopped there because of the cold. By all the saints, I have never known such piercing cold! The tremendous snows which fall in that mountainous wasteland kept us from even entering it."

Diaz paused, then went on with reluctance. "And more than that, Your Grace, I do not think Fray Marcos crossed the wilderness, either, to look on Cibola. I believe he went no farther than Red House, if indeed he went as far as that."

This statement came like a blow to Francisco. "Why do you say that, Captain?" he asked quickly.

"There are seven cities in that province, as the friar said. But Cibola is not the name of one. It is the name of the province. The place where Estevan was killed is called Hawikuh, a fact the friar seemed not to know. Also, none of the Indians with Estevan were killed, but all returned to their people. Furthermore, I do not think the friar had time to go so far."

Coronado was silent, thinking. Why would Fray Marcos have told an untruth, if he had? Yet Diaz was a man of honor and of great good sense. Who was right?

Captain Diaz continued. "It seems to be true that the natives of Cibola raise turkeys and grow beans and melons. They spin and weave cotton. They have many turquoises. But I could find no sign of silver or gold."

The two men sat in silence, looking at each other. Then Diaz rose to leave. "By the way, the warriors of Hawikuh have sent word to the Red House people to kill any strangers who come among them, or they will come and do it."

"If we repeat that news," Francisco replied drily, "no worthy son of Spain will turn back, gold or no gold."

The general kept Diaz's report to himself, but had Fray Marcos preach a sermon to refresh the spirits of his men. The friar's words were magic as he pictured again the fabulous cities with their walls of shimmering gold. Young grandees threw away costly articles to lighten their packs and speed the journey. The long-robed missionaries picked up their skirts in both hands, and with their knees thus freed for action, strode beside the jingling horses.

Francisco spurred his horse into place at the head of his forces. Melchior Diaz rode on one side of him, and Fray Marcos walked on the other. The army was once more on its way, and that was good.

But the general was troubled. Was Diaz right about Cibola? Or was Fray Marcos? He looked from one to the other. Whom was he to believe? All he could do was wait and see. It was a disturbing puzzle.

With spirits restored, the explorers were within two

leagues of Culiacan on March 28, the day before Easter. They were met by a committee of citizens of that outpost of empire bringing a strange request. Would they please not enter the town until Monday?

Coronado, although mystified, agreed to wait.

Monday morning as the troops approached the town they saw men waiting for them with horses and cannon in battle order! Hardly had the general time to ponder this when it became clear the skirmish was in fun. The settlers wanted the army to enter Culiacan as "conquerors"!

It was a delightful welcome, Francisco wrote to Mendoza and Doña Beatrice, especially as this would be the last contact with civilization. It was also a short relief from the two problems which vexed him most. He felt that the expedition had been moving too slowly, and he was worried about the food supply.

At the end of the week he called a meeting of his officers. On a day sweet with spring they sat on their booted heels under pale green trees and talked. The general turned first to Captain Tristan de Arellano, who was cousin to the viceroy. "Don Tristan, how much longer should the cattle rest and graze before we drive them on?"

"Two weeks, at least."

He asked Melchior Diaz, "How long before the harvest here is ready, that we may buy food?"

"Two or three weeks."

Francisco held up his hands in dismay. "We go so slowly, *señores!* It is my proposal to take a small group, lightly equipped and carrying the corn that is ready, and plunge ahead. The main army, with the herds, will follow as soon as is practical."

Tristan de Arellano was first to speak. "The plan is sensible."

Francisco saw the younger captains eye each other uneasily. He knew what was in their minds: all of them wanted to go with the vanguard. Garcia Lopez de Cardenas, who had been made army-master after the death of Samaniego, asked the question for all. "Who would be left in charge of the main army?"

"I was thinking of Captain Arellano," Coronado answered.

Arellano consented, and the younger men breathed easier. They would not be left out of adventure!

When the general left Culiacan, he had with him eighty Spaniards mounted on fast horses, and twenty-five tough foot-soldiers. He took the Franciscans, a few of the Indian allies, and rations for eighty days.

As they hurried along the ancient Indian trailway

to the north, they found the shelters of woven palms which the natives had erected for Fray Marcos the year before. Francisco saw the pleasure with which the Indians greeted him now. The doubts put into his mind by Melchior Diaz evaporated like the mists from the valleys.

Travel was easy here. The spring weather was comfortable. Men and horses were becoming tough and trail-wise. When they were able to barter with the Indians on the Sinaloa River for a little corn, the general and Captain Cardenas figured they had enough food to take them to Hawikuh, if all went well.

But as they approached the Rio Fuerte, the jungles of the coastal plain gave way to desert country. The heat made sword hilts burn the hand. Thorny mesquite and cactus reached out to tear the packs from mules and horses. Francisco shuddered to see the golden corn spilled and trampled into the golden sand. But they crossed the Fuerte with their hopes still bright and their laughter strong.

They pressed on without stopping until they came to Vacapa. This was the village where Fray Marcos and Estevan had parted the year before, where the friar had had his last sight of the black man. Francisco saw that the Indians remembered the friar with veneration. They brought their sick to him to be healed. They touched the garments of all the Franciscans with a shy homage which the general knew would please Doña Beatrice. He must remember to tell her about it.

Last year this tribe had given the friar and the Moor a supply of preserved prickly pear. This year they had none to give. So Coronado ordered a quick march on to the Mayo River.

He asked Fray Marcos, "How is the trail from here, Father?"

"Good! Good roads and beautiful green country," the friar replied. Francisco looked from his round face with its confident and friendly smile to the scowling Melchior Diaz, who was shaking his head. He was more than a little annoyed at the rugged mayor for doubting Fray Marcos.

But the next part of their way turned out to be so rough they had to cut new trails to get through it. Francisco found his own faith in Fray Marcos beginning to waver. Even the plain soldiers grumbled at their guide.

Captain Cardenas observed sourly, "One wonders what sort of roads he has traveled to call this good."

"This makes me believe," Melchior Diaz stated firmly, somewhat stubbornly, "that he went no farther than Vacapa, but put into his report what the Indians had told him. I believe they failed to tell him of these rocky forests. Farther on we shall find that beautiful green country. It is the Yaqui Valley."

Then they broke out of the mountains into the fertile valley of the Yaqui River, and Francisco saw that Diaz was right. Still he excused the friar. It would have been easy to forget.

This valley was the home of the southern Pimas — well-built, well-dressed Indians, friendly and generous. But the Pimas had no food to spare. They would have maize later, but it had not ripened under the rainless sky. By this time the explorers had only a little corn meal in their saddlebags. There was nothing left for the tired horses.

Wearier and hungrier than they had been yet, they found the same story at Matape. Rain had been too scant to ripen the beans and squash.

The general hastened on, promising his men a rest at Corazones, in the Sonora Valley. When at last they could see the Sonora River spreading its silver ahead of them, the weary explorers took a deep breath and a new grasp on their courage to reach it. Ten horses had died on that hard journey.

The general's face was haggard and sunburned, his eyes dark with fatigue. The golden armor had long since been packed away in favor of leather jacket and breeches. But that first night outside of Corazones, as he walked about among his men, cheering them as he could, he himself was cheered by the respect and affection he met. His men were a real army now, bound together by the hardships they had shared.

They had come five hundred miles from Culiacan in a month and four days. They were now, on May 26, fifteen hundred miles from Mexico City. An unknown number of miles and days stretched ahead of them into an unknown future.

Curbing his impatience, Francisco stayed in Corazones four days. The Pimas here had a system of irrigation which had saved their crops. Moreover, they were generous and shared their corn. For a few days the general could forget the gnawing worry of starvation.

This was the friendliest tribe the Spaniards had yet visited. Francisco could understand why the village had been the favorite of Cabeza de Vaca, who had named it *Villa de Corazones,* or Town of Hearts, because he and Estevan and the two captains had been given hundreds of dried deer hearts on their southward journey. Now the Pima men helped pasture the horses and stock. The women and children peeped out shyly from the mud and cobble houses. The women wore soft deerskin skirts and

jackets. The dark-eyed children wore hardly more than a look of happiness.

Through interpreters among the Mexican Indians, these Pimas told of the visit of Cabeza de Vaca and his three companions, and of Estevan's return last year. Whether they remembered Fray Marcos, Francisco could not tell. They treated him with the same reverence they gave to all the friars.

The Spaniards were most curious about the strings of turquoises the redmen wore, the number seeming to depend on their standing in the tribe. The chieftain, a dignified old man, wore many ropes of them. He told them the stones came from the walled towns of the north.

Would the Pimas send guides to show them the way? the general asked. When the chieftain agreed, Cibola, somehow, seemed closer. Even the mountain barrier, which must still be crossed, seemed less awesome.

Puerta de Oro, the Spaniards named the pass through the mountains, and Doorway of Gold it seemed to Coronado and his followers. It was only a small opening cut by the Sonora River not far from Corazones, but it took them through the mountain wall.

For the next thirty miles the trail led upward through rugged gorges which lay like huge folded pleats on the land. Men and horses breathed hard from the strain of climbing. The explorers felt repaid, however, when they reached the upper Sonora Valley, one of the most beautiful parts of Mexico. Long and narrow, it shimmered green between its dark sierras. Villages of the Opata Indians dotted the irrigated fields. Like patterns in a rug, Francisco thought.

Here, too, there was food, and the general was tempted to linger. But Hawikuh in Cibola was the goal, and time was passing. He ordered the troops on.

Following now their Opata guides, they again threaded a deep and narrow canyon. Horses slipped and stumbled while crossing and recrossing the stream. In the next valley they found Arizpe, an old town, in a vale as lovely as any in the Spanish homeland.

After Arizpe, the Spaniards left the Rio Sonora. For the next four days the trail-toughened army crossed a grassy tableland. It was hot and unpeopled. The first river they reached on the other side gave them a surprise. Instead of flowing south, as all the others had, it flowed to the north. They had crossed the continental divide, a short distance below the present border of the United States and Mexico. Somewhere along this north-flowing river, which was probably the San Pedro, they came into what is now Arizona.

They were in a land like nothing they had seen before, or even imagined. Francisco felt as if he were riding through a dream. Snakes and Gila monsters left their tracks in the sand between spiny cactus and gray-green sage. Beyond the mesquite and creosote bushes rose strange, flat-topped mesas. Weirdest of all in this weird country were the mirages. Only Melchior Diaz and his scouts did not view the disappearing vistas of water with cries of amazement.

More and more of the Spaniards began to wonder why Fray Marcos had not told them of these things. One was Fray Juan de Padilla, the toughest of the Franciscans. Lean and tireless, he often walked in the van beside the horses of Coronado, Diaz, and Captain Cardenas. He had been a soldier in his youth and knew soldiers' talk and soldiers' ways. But what struck Francisco most was the friar's boundless curiosity, especially about the Indians and the way they lived.

While they were among the northern Pimas, Fray Juan pointed out to the general how they reminded him of the Moroccan people of Africa. The women painted their eyes and chins in a Moorish fashion. And in the evenings the chieftain ascended a small mound to shout his proclamations in the manner of public criers of Europe.

"It is hard for me to realize we are in the midst of barbaric tribes in the outlands of New Spain," Fray Juan marveled.

As the sweating men pressed on through the rugged Galiuro Mountains of Arizona and across the high Arivaipa valley, Fray Juan asked Captain Diaz about Red House. "What shall we find there?"

Diaz only smiled and shook his head and said, "Wait and see."

"Now you sound like Fray Marcos," Juan de Padilla said, with a twinkle in his eyes.

Then, at the foot of a pass near the Gila River, they found an ancient rust-colored fortification almost crumbled away from the mountainside to which it clung.

"This is Red House," Melchior Diaz told them. He sat his horse with a half-smile on his weathered face, watching the surprised expressions of his comrades. They had all expected something more than this aged reminder of times long past.

Francisco watched, too, and with a heavy heart he saw that Fray Marcos was as surprised as the rest. He knew now that Melchior Diaz was right. That puzzle was solved. But there remained the mystery of why Fray Marcos had falsified his report. Even now, more than four hundred years later, there is still no answer to that question.

4

Camp
of
Death

Francisco dismounted from his big chestnut horse. He wanted to explore these mysterious red ruins. But he was smiling to himself at the exclamations of his comrades, thinking how typical they were. With him, besides Melchior Diaz, Fray Juan de Padilla, and Captain Cardenas, were two of his favorite captains, Hernando de Alvarado and Pedro de Tovar.

Young Captain Alvarado had disdain in his voice as he muttered, "This roofless old relic is the place we've heard so much about!" His dismay was brief, however, and gave way to his usual eagerness. "There's nothing here, Don Francisco. Let's get on."

Captain Cardenas thought of the horses. "The grass here is green and plentiful. Let's give our mounts time to graze and rest."

Francisco smiled at both of them. He had come to love these two as his brothers, but how different they were! Cardenas, taking time to think and be thorough, was sometimes too slow for the general's impatience. Alvarado, on the other hand, had less patience even than Francisco. He was always hurrying him on, always eager to know what lay ahead. "They keep me in good balance," Francisco thought, and was grateful for both.

Restless Juan de Padilla was already poking around in the fallen red-earth walls. A faraway look was in his eyes. "It makes you wonder . . . so lonely now . . . but people of some sort built it. What sort? And when? And where did they go, and why?

Captain Tovar was as practical as he was plump and genial. He sighed and said, "They left too long ago to do us any good in the matter of food. Our supply, you know, is very low again."

Then Melchior Diaz spoke. "There are natives close by, a rather miserable lot, but friendly. Or so they were last winter. Shall I call them out of hiding?"

"Yes, find them," Coronado replied. "Ask them if they have food for barter."

44

Captain Cardenas lifted a hand. "Wait a moment. I've been thinking about our ships. Fray Marcos reported that the coast is only fifteen miles from Red House. If we ever have need of those supplies, it is now. They may be in this neighborhood."

The general nodded. "Splendid idea. Captain Diaz, will you also ask for guides to the sea?"

Diaz turned to leave. Francisco chuckled to himself to see the tall padre stride off beside him. "Try to keep Fray Juan away from heathens! By the way, where is Fray Marcos?"

"He is back with the Mexican Indians," Cardenas answered.

By the time the rest of the troops had come up and the horses were grazing, Diaz and Juan de Padilla returned. Their faces were set in gloom. "There is no food for barter," they reported. "And the sea is not fifteen miles from here, but fifteen days."

"Fifteen days!" Coronado echoed in surprise. "We can't stay here that long."

Captain Alvarado jumped into his saddle. "Let's go on. There should be enough wild game in the wilderness to keep us alive."

"And don't forget," Melchior Diaz put in, "the Cibolanos want to kill us. If we wait here, they will learn of our presence and attack us. Our best plan is to surprise and attack them."

"Surprise them, yes," Coronado said firmly, "but attack only if our efforts at peace fail. But we shall camp here tonight."

For the first time the general prepared his force to enter hostile territory. Armor was unpacked. Lances were tested. The strongest horses were chosen for the saddles. Fifteen of the best men, under Cardenas and Alvarado, were sent out early next morning to keep a day's ride ahead of the squadron. They were to hunt for meat, select camp sites, and be alert for signs of ambush.

That night at Red House Francisco lay awake for a long time. Fray Marcos, he was now certain, had taken the word of the Indians for much that he reported, and had often either misunderstood or been deceived. If he had not looked upon Hawikuh, as he claimed, how far wrong would his report on Cibola turn out to be? Were there any golden walls? What if there were not even enough gold to repay the cost of the expedition? Would his men mutiny if they must return empty-handed? What would the king do? And the viceroy?

As he lay looking at the stars, Francisco wondered what thoughts were in the mind of Fray Marcos. Was it fear of the soldiers that made him remain with the

Indian allies? The friar was the only man Francisco would not have traded places with that night.

Next day, on June 23, Coronado led the rest of his vanguard through a gap in the Piñaleno mountains now called Eagle Pass. They crossed the Gila River into the last and worst part of their long pull to Cibola.

Excitement helped overcome fatigue. Soon, now, soon they would know! Even though Francisco had steeled himself to expect but little treasure from the seven cities, he still held a faint hope he might be wrong.

After the Gila River, they forded Ash Creek and Salt River. For five days they plodded upward through tooth-like mountains. There had been no grass for the horses since they left the Gila River. The gaunt-ribbed beasts were growing weaker every day.

The men fared but little better, living on a handful of dried corn each day. The hunters had not been successful in finding meat. The mountain sheep and the few other animals they saw were too fast and too far away to be brought down.

The threat of starvation, so close to their goal, was again heavy on Coronado's heart and mind. Leaning wearily against the sweaty withers of his horse, he looked backward to see the troops still coming on. Men were walking to spare the tired animals. He could not see the end of them, strung out thinly to the south. The rear guard was hidden by juniper-grown boulders which overhung the trail.

The general wiped his face before turning to Captain Tovar. "It is time we rested, Don Pedro, no?"

"Time, indeed, Don Francisco. No rest since morning. But you were right. No point in stopping until we found shade, or grass, or food . . . " His voice trailed away. There was still no grass nor food, only shade. He, too, gazed down the line of men. The nearer ones had stopped. They set to wiping down their dust-caked horses, massaging saddlesores and inspecting hoofs.

Tovar's smile was sad but proud. "Spain has borne hardy sons. Her harsh mountains have trained them well for these still wilder ones."

The general nodded. "There is only one thing our true Spaniard fears, Don Pedro."

"And that?"

"Labor."

Pedro de Tovar shook with his chuckle. "Yes! We'll endure any hardship to keep from working!"

Fray Juan de Padilla had walked up in time to hear the last words. He asked, "Did you ever consider, *Senores*, how much alike are the natives of Spain and America?"

Both men looked at the Franciscan with eyebrows raised. He explained, "Both have hardihood, pride, and a fierce love of personal freedom. Also a deep faith according to the knowledge of each."

Coronado added, "Also, I regret, an indifference to suffering."

Tovar said, "Yes, that's true of both. But remember, in themselves as well as in others."

"What do you think of the spirit of our men, Fray Juan?" the general asked.

"The same as with any army. There are those who are jolly and those who grumble. Some grumble because we go too fast, others because we're too slow. And you know" — he talked on, rubbing his forehead where his flat-crowned hat had left a mark — "I think the same struggle goes on in all our minds: curiosity tugging us onward, a dread of disappointment dragging at our heels."

Francisco placed a hand on the gray-robed shoulder. "Well put, Father. And I would add that good sense, like our good padre, strides ever back and forth between the two, holding the expedition together."

He had long ago decided there was enough courage in Fray Juan's bony frame for six men. Wherever there was trouble in the column, there he would be, giving a man a hand up a rocky ledge, holding another's horse, or putting down a sudden quarrel with a smile or a few words.

As sunset gave way to the sudden darkness of the mountain country, the expedition moved on. Coronado hoped to find food for the starving horses. Through half the glimmering night they walked, following the markers left by Captain Cardenas. The untouched land was more spectacular than ever in the radiance of moonlight shot with blue shadows. Only when the animals were too tired to travel farther did they make camp.

Soon after sunrise, Melchior Diaz, always scouting ahead and to the sides of the trail to see what he could find, returned to the general with a message from Captain Cardenas. Ahead lay a sweet-watered river with grass on its banks like the grass of Castile! Onward, then!

At the river the horses blew and rolled and cavorted with what strength they had. Some were so weak that the men had to pluck clumps of grass and feed them.

While they were lashing logs together to make rafts to cross this stream, the Spaniards decided to call it Rio de las Balsas. Today it is called the White River.

Since there was still no food for the men, they pushed on. They crossed two more small streams and entered a forest of majestic pine trees. They were in the

Mogollon Forest. All day they walked in quietness, their footfalls deadened by the fallen pine needles. Even the most talkative soldiers were quiet in the churchlike dimness.

Toward evening they found the scouting party waiting for them in what seemed a tiny paradise. A cool spring gurgled from a ledge of rocks at the foot of the pines. All around was grass. The men found some watercress to eat.

Robust Juan Gallego, commander of the rear guard, chewed with a look of distaste and snorted, "Are we little nibbling hares that our stomachs crave this dainty greenery?"

"Hares," murmured Coronado. "Captain Gallego, contain yourself with patience. Perhaps we shall yet find some of the hares and partridges Fray Marcos claimed for this wilderness."

"Your Grace," the captain protested, "you know we have seen nothing but the flash of a puma or the quicker flash of a mountain goat."

"Ah, yes," Coronado sighed. Truly too much had not been as the friar had told them.

But the night beside the spring passed with more comfort than many which had gone before.

It seemed to the general he had hardly closed his eyes when the dawn bugle sounded—muted and soft lest its echoes reach Hawikuh. He was splashing cold water on his face, from a basin held by a young orderly, when Captain Tovar came up.

"Your pardon, Don Francisco," the captain said, with a grimness unusual for him, "but there is bad news. The soldier Espinosa is dead. His friends tried to waken him, thinking he slept overhard, but all life is gone."

"Take me to him," Francisco said quickly. He started after Tovar with water still glistening on his beard. They met Juan Gallego running toward him.

"Your Grace," Gallego panted, "two of the Negro servants died during the night!"

Francisco quickened his steps. "How weird that death has come among us so quietly, here in this place where we might least expect it, this cool arroyo with its sweet spring. What reason . . . ?"

Captain Gallego broke in. "One of the Indians from Sonora believes they ate some of the wild parsnips which grow near the spring. They are poisonous."

How many more? Francisco wondered, and counted it fortunate that only three men were taken. A little later he stood with bowed head while Fray Juan de Padilla murmured the burial service.

When it was over, Captain Tovar commented, "The wonder is that the padres have not been called upon more often for this duty."

Captain Juan Gallego, for all his fifty years as tough and wiry as a mountain-bred youth, put new heart into Coronado by saying, "I credit our good fortune to the wisdom and energy of our commander."

Francisco was pleased, but replied modestly, "No,

the credit goes to all. And now that we approach the warriors of Cibola, we must be more vigilant then ever."

"As for me," Captain Alvarado said wryly, pulling in his belt, "I shall be glad to see a settlement. Be it friendly or hostile, it will have food. Let us leave this camp of death quickly."

5

Decision at Hawikuh

Again Coronado sent Alvarado and Cardenas with their scouts to keep a day's ride ahead, before he came on with the rest of his men. The trail led them out of the forest into open, rolling country. The general felt easier here, for there was less chance of ambush.

Next day he was walking to stretch his legs and save his horse. He paused at the sound of hurrying hoofs. Alvarado came galloping into view. He panted, "Captain Cardenas is camped on a river we call Rio Bermejo. Four men from Cibola came to us there last evening, making signs of peace. They said they came to welcome us, and promised to bring food tomorrow."

"Wonderful news!" Francisco replied. "Food means life or death to us now. If we get it without a fight, splendid!"

The youthful captain shook his head. "Captain Cardenas does not trust them. We think they may be spies. He sent two of them back to Hawikuh with crosses and words of peace. The other two he keeps until you come."

Coronado ordered his men to make double time. He was curious to see these men and anxious to make a try for peace. Before the sun was gone, they reached the camp set up by the army-master on the Rio Bermejo, later called the Little Colorado.

The general spoke a soft greeting to the two stocky Indians while looking them over from headbands to leggings. "They appear to be sturdy and intelligent," he said to Fray Juan, "but I had expected them to be more warlike."

"Beware of their pride," Fray Juan cautioned. "See how it controls even their curiosity. Men will do much to protect such pride."

Francisco took note that the men looked straight at him, without glancing away at the horses, strange as these must have been to them. "Give them some rosary beads, Father, and see what they do."

The Cibolanos accepted the gifts with no change

of expression, only some murmured words. Then they slipped away into the hills.

"Peace or war?" Francisco asked.

Fray Juan de Padilla answered with the lift of a bony shoulder.

The general sent the scouts ahead once more, then followed with his troops. They were in what is now New Mexico, traveling along the north bank of the Zuñi River. Shortly before dusk they came to a good camping place and found Captain Cardenas waiting.

"We have talked with more of the Cibolanos, Don Francisco," he reported. "They seem friendly. But there is a narrow pass up ahead where they could ambush us. I left some men there to guard it."

Francisco dismounted and stretched. "Well done, Don Garcia. Should trouble come, call us with your bugle."

After Captain Cardenas rode away, the Spaniards made camp without fire or tents. The general loosened the girth of his big chestnut's saddle and lay down nearby with his boots still on. Tired as he was, he was too excited to sleep on this last night before reaching their journey's goal. His mind swung back and forth between memories of home and awareness of danger ahead. He could see the black hills flickering with signal fires and knew that the men of Cibola were not sleeping either. But no sound came to indicate their actions. The earth was as silent as the starry sky.

Suddenly Francisco jumped to his feet. His ears had caught echoes of shouts and yells. Before he heard the bugle call he was ready to ride. "Hurry!" he ordered the men around him.

The tumult was over by the time they had clattered up to the pass.

Captain Cardenas, hearing them, called out quickly, "All is well!" Then he came up and said, "But for a while I didn't know. They surprised us completely. All was so quiet I let the men unsaddle, except for two mounted sentries."

At that moment Captain Alvarado pulled rein beside the general. He was out of breath but laughing. "Did you ever hear such a noise as those Indians made? Like ten thousand devils! Some of our horses bolted. And some of the soldiers got as rattled as the horses and threw their saddles on hind part before!"

Cardenas was still serious. "It didn't take us long to run them off, once we got over the surprise."

"Then it is to be a fight at Hawikuh, I think," said Francisco thoughtfully.

The Spaniards were on the march, fully armed,

when sunrise of Wednesday, July 7, filled the eastern sky. As they neared Hawikuh, they caught glimpses of the Cibolanos spying on them from rocky crevasses. Francisco could feel his muscles grow tense under the golden armor he had put on to enter Cibola. With tight rein he followed Captain Cardenas and his two Opata guides into the narrow Zuñi valley. He kept a wary eye on Captain Alvarado and Melchior Diaz, riding point on either side with spears in hand.

The general's ear was attuned to sounds in the lines behind him, the short, sharp orders which betrayed the mounting excitement of his followers. Now and again he turned to look back. Following the cavalry, the foot soldiers kept their crossbows trained on the hillsides. Behind them came the rear guard under Juan Gallego. Far enough back to stay out of any fighting were the Mexican Indians and Fray Marcos. The other friars walked with the infantry.

The valley widened, and the trail turned. Captain Cardenas stopped with uplifted arm. The general and his officers spurred to join him. Then they all stopped and looked. There, at the foot of a brown hill, was Hawikuh, the key to their fortunes, the reason for the expedition.

Francisco blinked. Even in his most pessimistic moments, he had expected more than this! True, the houses were three and four stories high, all built together one on top of another. But the pueblo looked mean and squat, as dun-colored as the earth it sat on. Nothing about it sparkled or spoke of treasure.

"It looks all crumpled up," Melchior Diaz said plaintively, as if he could not believe what he saw.

"I have seen peasant houses in Spain that are better than this," said Alvarado, dismayed.

"Grander than Mexico, Fray Marcos called it," Cardenas snorted. There was such cold anger in his voice that Francisco feared for the safety of the friar.

But that was a fleeting thought. More important right now were the warriors standing in military order outside the walls of the town. More than two hundred, Coronado estimated quickly. They were armed with bows and arrows and war clubs, and wore shields and jackets of leather, brightly painted. The men were short, but stocky and strong, brave looking in their defiance.

"Why do they keep dancing and pointing to the ground?" Coronado asked his Opata interpreter, an old man who had lived in Cibola as a boy.

"On the ground they have made a line with sacred corn meal," the old Indian explained. "They order you not to cross it."

The general signaled for his secretary, Bermejo, to ride up close to him. Bermejo was to read to the Indians the "requirement" of King Charles, as was the Spanish custom in new lands. "Ride beside him, Don Garcia," Coronado said to Captain Cardenas. "Fray Luis and Fray Daniel will go before you on foot."

While the valiant Franciscans stood by the head of his horse, Bermejo read from a long parchment held before him on his saddle. If the Indians would submit peacefully to the rule of the great emperor across the water, it was proclaimed, no harm but much good would come to them.

The Cibolanos waited restlessly for Bermejo to finish. But when the old Opata began translating the long Spanish sentences, the red warriors drowned out his voice with a great shout and let fly a shower of arrows. Bermejo's horse squealed and reared, with a shaft in his neck. Fray Luis, not retreating a step, bent down to pull one from the skirt of his cassock.

Before the Indians could shoot again, Coronado, eye-catching in his golden armor and plumed helmet, trotted to the front, almost to the sacred line. The gifts he held out in both hands were disdained by the stubborn Cibolanos, who were keen for battle. Behind him his own men were loudly urging him to fight.

"Hold!" he ordered sternly. Not until the formalities were ended would he give battle orders. He asked his interpreter, "What do the men of Cibola shout at us?"

"They call you cowards," he was told.

This was too much for Spanish pride. The general looked at the Franciscans. They nodded approval. He had done all that he could for peace. Swinging his sword high, he turned to the soldiers. "St. James and at them!" he shouted.

Echoing his *Santiago,* the old Spanish war cry, the horsemen spurred furiously toward the walls of the town. "St. James and at them!" The Indians on the plains broke and ran. The horsemen chased after. But some of the exhausted beasts stumbled and fell. From the terraced roofs came such a bombardment of arrows and stones that the others were forced to pull back.

"We must dismount!" Coronado cried, and shouted out new orders. The crossbowmen and arquebusiers were to drive the Indians from the terraces while the cavalry, afoot, stormed the gate.

"St. James and at them!" The rush for the gate gathered force behind Coronado. Still the arrows and stones came pelting down. The infantry could not budge the natives from their rooftops. The sun-rotted strings of their crossbows snapped at the first shots. The arquebusiers were almost too weak to hold their heavy, slow-firing guns.

"Don't give up!" the general shouted. His bright armor made him an easy target. He was hit in the face with a stone, but recovered his balance. They were pushing through the gate when an arrow struck him in the foot. He kept on fighting. But suddenly there was the thud of a large stone against his helmet. The blow set him reeling, and the world went dark.

The next thing Francisco knew, he woke in his tent with Fray Juan de Padilla sitting beside him. "Lie still," the padre said. "The battle is over. Hawikuh has surrendered to Captain Cardenas."

"What about food?" Francisco asked. His voice surprised him by its weakness.

"There are great quantities in the first-floor rooms which we may have. Piñon nuts, dried deer and turkey meat, beans, and yellow maize which our men think more beautiful right now than yellow gold."

"What of our casualties?"

"Your injuries are the most severe. You would have been killed, so intent were the Indians upon you, had not Cardenas and Alvarado stood over you until you could be moved. They received bruises while protecting you. Four men have arrow wounds. Three horses were killed."

"What of the warriors of Hawikuh?"

"They lost ten or twelve. The others asked permission to leave the pueblo, even though Captain Cardenas told them they would be safe here. They wanted to join their women and children, who had been taken to hiding places in the cliffs before we came. Many of the braves had come from the other pueblos of Cibola and wanted to go home."

"We must try to make them our friends now," Francisco muttered, and went back to sleep.

6

The
Turquoise
Towns

In the morning the general rose as soon as the sun shone through the door of his tent. He examined himself in a polished silver mirror. Yes, his face looked as bruised and swollen as it felt! He tried to walk and winced with pain. But after Fray Juan de Padilla fashioned a cane for him, he was able to get about.

And get about he must, for there was much to do. He inspected the Spanish camp outside the walls of the town. "Well done," he told the army-master. He sent word to the Cibolanos that they would not be disturbed when they came out to tend their gardens.

Then he invited the head men of the tribe to visit him. He was still too bruised to wear his shining armor, but the golden helmet made a lordly crown. He seated himself in the sunshine outside his tent, with a few of his officers standing behind him.

The chieftains came wearing so many turquoise necklaces, bracelets, and belts that their deerskin clothing was almost covered. They wore headbands around their black hair, which was cut in bangs. They greeted the Spaniards with sober courtesy. No one spoke of the battle.

Captain Alvarado, with a great show of ceremony, gave each chieftain some pieces of colored Venetian glass and a string of little tinkling bells. The Cibolanos, in turn, laid at the general's feet their gifts of woven blankets, deer hides, and polished turquoises. As Francisco spilled the blue-green stones from one hand to the other, he turned to Captain Cardenas. "Not the treasure we expected, eh? But let us get together some things of this land to send the viceroy. May I see one of the hides?"

He crushed the soft, cream-colored deerskin in his hand; it felt like silken velvet. "We must learn the secret of their tanning." Then he looked at the designs painted on it in delicate colors. "Ask the Cibolanos," he requested the old Opata interpreter, "if they will paint for me two such skins, showing the animals and birds of this province."

"Yes, yes." The Indians nodded and smiled. His interest seemed to please them.

More, he thought to himself, than their information pleased him. None of the chieftains knew the difference between silver, brass, gold, and iron. All metals were strange to them. Coronado must be content that they had food to give, and pasture for the horses.

"Now," said the general through the interpreter, "I must scold you." They had done wrong, he said, in not giving obedience willingly to King Charles as he had requested. But if they would do so now, they would be forgiven. The chiefs promised obedience so quickly that he wondered if they understood. But it showed their willingness to be friends.

When gentle Fray Daniel told them about the church, they seemed to understand better. It was a strange thing to the Spaniards that so many Indians of the New World already had a reverence for the symbol of the cross. They promised to become Christians, and to bring their children to be baptized.

Next he asked about the death of Estevan. The oldest chieftain explained. "He came to us carrying the emblem of our enemies, a feathered gourd rattle. While we held a council about what to do, we put him in the small house outside the gate. But the black man tried to run away. Then our warriors shot him."

Then the youngest chieftain sang for the Spaniards a song-story they had made up about the black Mexican who had come from the Land of Everlasting Summer. "It will be taught to our children and our children's children," he said. His words were true. The legend is still sung in the pueblos of Zuñi-land in New Mexico.

"What of the Indians who came with the black man?" Coronado asked. "Were they killed?"

The Cibolanos were shocked. "Oh, no, they were not hurt. All were sent back to the Land of Everlasting Summer."

Francisco looked at his fellow Spaniards and saw his own thought reflected. Melchior Diaz had been right about this, too, and Fray Marcos wrong.

The Opata continued to translate the Indian's statement. "Lest our story of the man as black as night be not believed, we sent pieces of his body to our other five towns. Also his green dishes . . ."

Coronado interrupted. "Other five towns? Are there not seven in this kingdom?"

The Indian said, "In our land, six. In Tusayan there are seven."

Captain Tovar asked quickly, "And where lies Tusayan?"

The Indians pointed to the northwest.

"It will bear investigation, Don Francisco, no?" the captain asked, with brows lifted in hopeful expectation.

Coronado lowered his eyes. What could he say? With all his heart he had hoped to start home within a week. But had he done his full duty? His words came out slowly. "I think nothing would be found there, either, Don Pedro."

Exclamations of protest from all the captains stopped him. Cardenas said earnestly, "I trust in God that if any gold is to be found, it shall not escape us for lack of diligence."

Francisco eased himself erect with the help of his cane. He felt a hundred years old. "I will think about it," was all he could bring himself to say as he walked away. After darkness had covered Hawikuh and the stars were out, he was still fighting the battle within himself. He sent for Fray Juan. With the friar's help he walked to a small mound and sat with his face to the heavens.

"What am I to do, Father?" he asked. "All my feelings and all my desires urge me homeward. We have done that which we set out to do. We have made the kingdom of Cibola a part of Spain. Is it now my duty to search farther for treasure? Must we stay until all this land is known to us?"

"It is not for me to tell you, my son," Fray Juan answered kindly. "Your own conscience must make the decision."

Francisco knew what the decision must be, yet he dreaded admitting it. Of course he must stay, and he must search. He owed it to all those who had put their faith in him and their money into the expedition. He owed the Franciscans a chance to work with the heathen.

Next day Captain Tovar started out for Tusayan. With him were seventeen mounted men, three foot-soldiers, some Zuñi guides, and Fray Juan de Padilla. They were to return within thirty days.

Then Francisco set himself to writing messages to be sent to Mexico City. He had written Doña Beatrice by his own hand. But for the long report to the viceroy he called in the secretary, Bermejo. Making himself comfortable on a couch of braided rabbit skins, he dictated the details of the hard march to Cibola and of the battle. "Because my armor was gilded and glittered I was hurt more than the rest, not because I had done more; for these gentlemen and soldiers bore themselves well, as was expected of them," he had Bermejo write.

"It now remains for me to tell about the Seven Cities of which Fray Marcos gave your Lordship an account. I can assure you he has not told the truth in a single thing he has said except the name of the kingdom and the large stone houses." After listing the objects he was sending, Coronado continued, "I wish I had better news to write Your Lordship, but I must tell you the truth, the bad as well as the good." He paused for a long time, sighed, nodded to Bermejo, and went on. "Nor shall I think of ceasing my efforts until death overtakes me, if it serves His Majesty or Your Lordship to have it so. I shall suffer every hardship rather than abandon this enterprise."

Later, when his officers in a council meeting repeated this pledge with him, Francisco knew that his course was set on the path of duty, with no turning back.

Planning, then, for the future, Coronado thought of this new land as a giant chessboard. It stretched from Culiacan on the south to unknown boundaries on the north, east, and west. He must move his men over it with the utmost care lest he lose them. Captain Tovar was exploring westward. Captain Arellano and the main army should by now be somewhere in the Sonora Valley, moving northward.

Already he could see that Cibola would not support the entire expedition. If Arellano were to leave part of his forces in the Sonora Valley, perhaps at Corazones, that would divide the food problem, and also give a halfway base for messengers. After much thought, Coronado chose Melchior Diaz to take the orders to Arellano, and to remain as commander of the post to be set up. His first task would be to search for the supply ships.

He chose another of the older men, the sturdy Juan Gallego, to carry the precious letters and objects to Mexico City. He charged him, too, with another duty. He was to return to Cibola with a pack train of food and supplies as quickly as he could.

"It means a hard, man-tiring ride of three thousand miles," Coronado told Gallego. "But if any man can do it, you are the one."

Gallego assured him, "You may count on me, Your Grace. I shall return with supplies, come what may."

Diaz and Gallego were to go together as far as Corazones. With them when they started out were Fray Marcos and thirty of the Mexican Indians who wanted to go home. The friar did not think it wise for him to remain in Cibola, seeing the way the Spaniards had turned against him. Francisco agreed.

Soon after Diaz and Gallego left, Pedro de Tovar and Fray Juan de Padilla were back from Tusayan. They had found the home of the Hopi Indians. "Their villages," Captain Tovar reported, "are built on the ridges of red mesas, from which they descend to work their fields and get water. Otherwise they live much like the people of this pueblo."

"Were they friendly or hostile?" Coronado asked.

"Hostile at first, and plucky! Even though we surprised them, they quickly formed battle orders, drew their line with the sacred corn meal, and dared us to cross. Then, after I read the 'requirement,' one of them struck my horse with his club. At that we shouted the *Santiago* and chased them back to their town."

Fray Juan broke in. "We learned later that they thought the horses ate people. Which makes their courage more remarkable."

"Soon the headmen came out with gifts," Captain Tovar went on. "They promised obedience to the king.

"Before the day was done, natives from the other Tusayan pueblos came to see us. They want us to visit them, to buy, sell, and barter. They have beautiful weaving, dressed skins, piñon nuts and, as everywhere in these towns, turquoises."

"No gold or silver?"

The captain and the friar looked at each other, then spoke together. "None, Don Francisco."

"What did you hear of the country farther on, toward the coast?"

"Nothing of interest, except that there is a great

river," Tovar replied. "The Indians say its like is not to be found anywhere on earth."

Captain Cardenas, frowning earnestly, was drawing a rough map on the ground. "If it is so large, might it not be an arm of the sea? Perhaps one that our ships might find?"

Captain Tovar studied the lines in the sand. "It might be possible, Don Garcia. But it would be a rugged journey to find out. The land is without water. When the Hopis go, they carry jars of water and bury them along the way for their return."

Captain Cardenas stood up and faced the west. "Then we could do the same. I should like to go there, Don Francisco."

So a few days later, on August 25, Captain Cardenas started for Tusayan with twenty-five horsemen to search for the big river. The infantry captain, Pablos de Melgosa, went along, but Coronado talked Fray Juan de Padilla into staying behind this time.

The lean friar's disappointment faded, a few days later, when he stood with Coronado to welcome some unusual visitors to their camp. The leader was tall, young and robust, friendly and talkative. He wore mustaches, a thing not often found among the redmen. Coronado immediately nicknamed him *Bigotes,* or Whiskers. An

older, smaller man he called *Cacique*, for Governor. He had a wonderful time talking with them, even through interpreters of interpreters and some sign language.

"We heard of strange, bold men who had come to this land," Bigotes boomed in his own tongue. "So from our pueblo of Pecos we have come to see for ourselves and to invite you to our country."

"Tell me about your country," the general urged. "But first tell me about this." He held before him a huge hide with tangled, woolly hair which Bigotes had brought him. "Truly I have never seen the like of it."

To explain the animal better, Bigotes called in one of his men who had a buffalo painted on his body. It set the curiosity of the Spaniards aflame. Pedro de Tovar went up close to the native for a good look. "You know, Don Francisco, these must be those humpbacked cattle Cabeza de Vaca and Estevan told us about. I must confess I thought they were stretching the truth."

A sudden gleam came into his eyes, but before he could say a word, Captain Alvarado jumped up and slapped him on the shoulder. "Ah, Don Pedro! I know what you are thinking! What hunting if we could go after a few of these monsters, no?" He flung himself on the ground beside Coronado. "Don Francisco, don't you think Pecos would bear investigation?"

By the time the laughter had died down, Bigotes had learned what they were saying. He spread both arms wide. "East of my village these cattle are thicker than leaves in a forest. Would you like to see them? We will guide you."

Four days later Coronado was saying good-by to Captain Alvarado and twenty companions. Every Spaniard still in Hawikuh stood with him to watch the little band start eastward.

Pedro de Tovar sighed. "How wonderful to be young! Look at them! They've already forgotten the hunger and harshness of the wilderness."

Francisco smiled. He was only thirty himself, but he felt older than any of them because of his cares. "It is just as well, Don Pedro. But think of Father Padilla. With all his years, he was even more eager to go than Don Hernando. He will hunt souls as zestfully as the others hunt the humpbacked cattle."

Although the friar was just back from the journey with Captain Tovar, he strode out of sight beside Alvarado's big bay horse. He had learned to walk as fast as an Indian or a horse. Four more of the Spaniards went on foot, carrying crossbows. The men from Pecos, dignified and pleased, led the way.

7

A
Tantalizing
Tale

Some two weeks later Coronado was surprised to receive a courier from the dashing Captain Alvarado, bearing a letter. "I am amazed that Don Hernando sat still long enough to write me," he said to Captain Tovar. "This is sent from a place he calls Tiguex. Let us see what is so important."

He read aloud from the letter. "After traveling through country black and harsh with volcanic lava, we came to the queerest sight in these new lands: a sandstone mesa rising abruptly from the level plain. On top is a sky city called Acoma. The only way up or down is by toe and finger holes cut in the rocks. It is a marvel how the women climb it with jars of water on their heads.

"Fray Juan says it is the greatest stronghold in the world. The people were friendly and came clambering down to meet us. But if they had spared themselves the trouble, and remained on their rock, we would not have been able to disturb them in the least. We gave them parrot feathers and hawk's bells in return for buffalo skins and cotton cloth.

"Three days' journey east of Acoma, we came to the River of Our Lady, as we named it. It flows through wide, serene green valleys with snow-covered mountains to the east. We camped on the south side of this province of Tiguex, which has twelve pueblos."

This was the valley of the Rio Grande on its southward course through New Mexico, with the Sangre de Cristo range towering above it. Tiguex lay north of present Albuquerque, above Bernalillo.

The letter went on, "The Tiguas seem to be more devoted to agriculture than to war. Food is abundant everywhere: maize, beans, melons, and turkeys. The people clothe themselves in cotton and the skins of cattle and have coats of turkey feathers. They are happy and friendly. From all the twelve towns they came to greet us, marching around my tent to the music of a flute.

"Father Padilla and I, guided by Bigotes, returned the visits. Wherever we erected crosses, the Indians decorated them with roses and feathers and worshipped as Father Padilla showed them."

By the time Francisco came to the last of the letter, he was not surprised that Captain Alvarado suggested the army spend the winter in Tiguex. Juan de Padilla had added a note approving the idea.

"I approve it, too," Coronado said. "Indeed it seems a better province than Cibola. As soon as Captain Arellano comes from Sonora, we shall all go there. Unless, of course, Captain Cardenas brings news of something better in the west."

Captain Cardenas came riding back to Cibola before his time was up. As he dismounted before the Spanish camp, Francisco hobbled out to give him a warm embrace, anxious to ask what had gone wrong. Then he noticed the gleam, almost of mischief, in the eyes of his sober friend. With an arm around his shoulder he guided the captain to his tent. There they sat and cracked piñon nuts while Cardenas told of his journey.

"We went for twenty days through high, barren, sandy country. No settlements beyond Tusayan all the way to the river. We were hampered by the lack of water, although the Hopis were generous with food and guides. I should say there is no use to explore farther in that direction."

"But you must have found the big river, my thorough friend! Else you would not be back. Is there no chance, then, to get in touch with our ships?"

Captain Cardenas laughed in his dry way and walked to the door of the tent. He called to Pablos de Melgosa and two comrades waiting outside. "Without them to back up my words," Cardenas explained, "you would never believe me. Yes, we found the big river. Rather, we found its chasm. When we came upon its brink, without warning, it took our breaths away! We were suddenly

on the edge of the world. The land just stopped. Nor did it start again for miles and miles. In between, down in the bottom of the greatest canyon you can imagine—"

"Even greater than you can imagine!" the younger officer put in.

Coronado cocked an eyebrow at him. "Now, Captain Melgosa!"

"Truly it is," Cardenas protested. "That God could have wrought such a miracle strains belief. But there it is! And so aglow with color we could never tell the whole of that! The river lay at the bottom. We thought it about six feet across. The Indians told us it was a mile. These three men, whom we picked as the most agile, tried to find a way down to it. They were out of sight all day."

Melgosa took up the story. "And at that, we went only some third of the way, we think. Rocks which we judged to be the size of a man turned out to be taller than the highest tower in Seville."

Francisco listened to this with his eyes crinkled in a skeptical smile. Belief did not come easy to the first Europeans to see and hear about the Grand Canyon of the Colorado in Arizona. "Now, Don Garcia," he remonstrated, "are we so hard up for wonders?"

The four men who had seen the canyon insisted that every word was true.

The general gave in. "Then indeed it is a marvel. If there is anything that Don Garcia fails to reach the bottom of — well, I wish I might see it. But the business of the expedition comes first. I believe the east holds more promise."

In short order Captain Cardenas was on the road again. With a dozen riders and some of the Indian allies, he was on the way to the province of Tiguex, in the valley of the Rio Grande. There he was to prepare winter quarters for everyone in the expedition.

Francisco waited restlessly now for the coming of Arellano and the main army. He fretted that everyone was seeing the country but him. Pedro de Tovar had been to Tusayan. Cardenas, too, and then on to the Grand Canyon and now to the east. Captain Alvarado and Father Padilla had been up and down the fertile valley of the River of Our Lady, and now were somewhere in the country of the humpbacked cows.

While Coronado waited, the air of Cibola turned crisp with cold. Now, in November, there was a new bitterness to the wind. It would go hard with Arellano's men in the great wilderness with its sierras and forests. And the cattle and sheep would make the going worse.

Every day the general sent out scouts to see if the army drew near. The snow came before Arellano did — a heavy, blowing storm of it, lasting all day. The next day a scout reported he had seen the army. "The soldiers walk and the Indians ride the horses," he told Francisco with a puzzled frown.

Francisco was worried as well as puzzled. Could the redmen have risen up and overpowered the Spaniards? Then why did they come on? Although he was still stiff from his wounds, he decided to ride forth himself to meet the travelers. He took an escort of picked men ready for any action.

From the turn in the trail near Hawikuh, he could see the army plowing through the snow, men and horses looking black against its whiteness. Soon he could recognize Tristan de Arellano. And he could see for himself that the Indians were riding horses led by the soldiers.

Captain Arellano quickly explained: the Indians rode because they were too weak to walk! Being used to a warm climate, and dressed for it, they were more troubled by the cold than were the heavier-clad Spaniards. The general sent a courier back to camp with orders to build great fires and prepare warm food.

Food and rest soon had the newcomers warm and restored. When they were settled, and the stock put under night watch, Coronado and Arellano sat together talking. The weary captain stretched his long legs close to the fire.

"We set up our post in the valley of the Opata villages," the captain began. "There Captain Gallego and Melchior Diaz found us in September, and told us the disappointing news about Cibola. I left eighty men there with Diaz. Poor Don Melchior! They were the worst of the lot. But I know he can handle them.

"All the way here the natives were friendly, friendlier than Nature was. The wilderness almost put an end to us! It is a good thing we had no battle to fight at the end of the trail, as you did. But tell me, since the battle you've had no trouble here?"

"None," Francisco answered. "We have learned to get along with the Cibolanos very well. You know, they make the best *tortillas* I have ever tasted. An interesting people, Don Tristan. They worship water, because it makes the maize grow and sustains their life, and because their ancestors did. Still, I think the Franciscans are finding them easy converts. Tiguex, however, will be better for us. More room, more food. I had thought to take you there as soon as you arrived, but —"

"We need rest," Arellano finished. "The poor sheep! Their hoofs are worn off. We had to leave some behind."

"Suppose, then, I go ahead with my men and you bring your force on in twenty days."

Arellano agreed that was best.

After four months of easy living at Hawikuh, Coronado was delighted to hear the creak of saddle leather under him again and the blowing of the horses in the wintry air. When he reached the River of Our Lady, he turned north and followed its banks to a village named Alcanfor. He rode up wearing his white-plumed helmet.

Before the entrance to the village he saw Captain Cardenas and his men standing at attention. On the other side of the gate were Captain Alvarado and his men. He glanced swiftly at the faces of his two good friends. Both were smiling and proud.

With a flourish, Captain Cardenas motioned the general to follow him into the town. The terraced houses were empty and silent. Francisco frowned.

"Be at ease, Don Francisco," Cardenas said quickly. "It was done peacefully. I persuaded the residents to move in with friends in the other pueblos."

"You used no force?" Coronado asked.

"No. Only gifts and words. Isn't this better than camping outside the walls as we did at Hawikuh?"

The general relaxed. "Yes, indeed, Don Garcia. You have done well. Better even than I had hoped." Then he turned to Captain Alvarado, whose dark eyes flashed with excitement. Francisco could imagine the difficulty with which he restrained himself. "Now, Don Hernando, what is your news? Do you, too, have something to show me?"

Alvarado flung his arms wide, making his horse shy. "I have the best news yet! The prize of all gifts! Come with me!"

Francisco was both amused and annoyed by Captain Alvarado's air of secrecy. As he strode along with him toward the far end of Alcanfor he said. "Heaven help you, Don Hernando, if this is some prank."

"I swear to you, Don Francisco, that what you are to see will be the turning point of our expedition. Only a few of my men — and not even Don Garcia — know the full story of this."

By this time they had reached a large room, its thick walls without windows. Two Spaniards stood guard beside the leather-hung doorway. One of them gave the captain a lighted torch. He stooped to enter the room, and Francisco followed.

The light fell first on the two guards inside the cell. Then its beams picked out an Indian wearing leg-chains. Francisco jerked with surprise as he saw the face leering at him, fierce-eyed and hawk-nosed, topped with a stiff roach of hair. Alvarado moved the torch to a second Indian, also in chains. He was tattooed oddly around the eyes, giving him the look of a raccoon.

Coronado's anger flared. "Captain Alvarado, I trust you have good reason for this dark business?"

Without replying, the young officer shone the torch upon two more natives in chains. At sight of them Coronado caught his breath and let it explode. They were his friends from Pecos, the bewhiskered Bigotes and the old Cacique!

He grasped Alvarado by the shoulder, but before he could speak the captain told him quickly, "You will understand when I tell you what happened."

The general's eyes were flashing, and his voice was cold as he demanded. "Did not Bigotes do as he promised?"

"Oh, yes. He took us to Pecos, where his people greeted us with joy and music."

Coronado was impatient. "What about the country of the cows? Did he not guide you there?"

"Not himself. He said he was tired after traveling with us those fifty days. That is when he gave us these two slaves for guides. He had captured them on the plains where the humpbacked cattle roam."

"So now master and slave are imprisoned together," the general said stiffly.

Without answering, Alvarado held aside the leather curtain for Francisco. When they were out of hearing of the guards, the captain said in a tense whisper, "It was on the plains that the Turk told me his story. He is the one with the bristly hair. I call him Turk because he looks like one."

"So?" Coronado murmured.

Alvarado still whispered. "He knows of a province where there is gold! It is called Quivira."

Francisco studied his friend. Certainly he had never seen the young man so excited, yet so sure of himself. If what he said were true . . . With swift decision he told him, "Bring the Turk to my quarters tonight. And you had better have a good explanation for the chains, Don Hernando!"

That night the general scarcely took his eyes off the hawk-nosed Turk. He sat bent forward with his elbows on his knees, watching the Indian's expressive hands as he used sign language. He watched the Indian even when an interpreter spoke to translate his words.

Captain Alvarado could not sit still, but paced back and forth in the low-ceilinged room, watching the commander.

Proud and angry though he looked, the Turk spoke freely. "I am from Harahey," he said, "northeast of this place, beyond the buffalo plains, and beyond Quivira, where the gold is."

"Quivira," Francisco murmured, liking the music of the name.

"There is a river in that land, in Quivira, with fish as big as horses. The chiefs ride in canoes with colored sails, with twenty rowers on each side. The prows are spreading eagles carved from gold. The lord of the land takes his nap under a tree hung with thousands of tinkling golden bells. The plainest people eat from dishes beaten out of gold."

Coronado handed the Turk a vessel made of tin. "Like this?"

The Turk smelled it and shook his head with disdain. When shown the golden helmet, however, he smiled and said, "This! This is the metal they have in Quivira."

Then Coronado saw visions! Maybe this fierce pagan was, after all, the key he sought! Glittering words were not always true words, he knew, remembering Cibola. But this man's talk was so straight, so full of details! Cautious though he was, Francisco found it hard not to believe him.

"This is most interesting, Don Hernando," he said at last. "But I should like more evidence than one person's story."

Alvarado planted himself squarely in front of the general. "If Bigotes were not so stubborn, you would have certain proof! The Turk wore a bracelet of gold when he was captured. Bigotes has it. But neither he nor Cacique will admit it."

"What about the other Indian, the one with the raccoon eyes?"

"He is from Quivira and is called Sopete. But he will not talk. That is why I put chains on all four of them and brought them to you."

The general put his hands to his head. "And you have brought me a pretty problem. The bracelet is important, yes. But the chains — we shall reap trouble from them. Let us hope Quivira is worth it."

Alvarado said stubbornly, "Bigotes need only show

us the bracelet. Then we can set them all free."

Francisco rose at daybreak, with the problem of Bigotes like a burr in his mind, but with the vision of Quivira like a song in his heart. He went immediately to the quarters of Father Padilla, and told him the whole story. "Will you speak to Bigotes?" he asked the friar.

Fray Juan nodded, saying, "It is very important to the service of His Majesty that the truth about the rich country should be known."

Before long Fray Juan came to report to the General. "Bigotes denies everything. He says the Turk lies."

Coronado placed the prisoners in the care of Captain Cardenas. "Feed them well, treat them kindly, but do not let them get away."

Soon everyone at Alcanfor knew about the Turk and his golden armlet. Shivering in their stone-walled, unheated rooms, the explorers warmed themselves with talk of Quivira. They blew on cold hands and said that now they were on the right trail. They stamped freezing feet when they were on cattle guard and tried to hurry the spring so they could go searching once more. On to Quivira!

8

Smoke
and
Snow
at Arenal

Winter settled upon the Rio Grande Valley with a severity unknown to the men from Mexico and Spain. The thin cotton of the Indian allies and the thinner silk of the grandees were no protection against wind and snow. Metal armor only added to the chill.

Francisco saw the looks of envy and longing his explorers turned on the people of the pueblos, wrapped in their bright woolen blankets, their toes warm in snug moccasin boots. He knew something had to be done to avoid illness and trouble with the natives. So he sent for the chief of Moho, the largest of the Tiguex towns.

The Spaniards had nicknamed this chieftain Juan

Aleman, or John the German, because he reminded them of a German merchant in Mexico City. Francisco chuckled over what the merchant would think if he could see this namesake who wore his long dark hair in plaits down each side of his brown face. Shell and turquoise ornaments dangled from his ears and around his neck.

Coronado requested from Juan Aleman, in trade, three hundred pieces of woolen cloth.

The Tigua shook his head. "We have not that much in our province," he said, "as we weave only what we need. We of Moho will do what we can to help you, but I may speak only for my own pueblo. You must ask the chieftain of each village, and he will talk with his people. That is the way we govern ourselves."

The general was caught between the desperate needs of his men and the customs of the Indians. He decided that the quickest way was to send captains to each town.

He had learned enough about these pueblo tribes to caution the officers. "The Tiguas will treat us as we treat them. Be careful lest you offend them by insulting their beliefs and habits which are different from ours. Remember that already they distrust us because we keep Bigotes and Cacique in prison."

A captain whom Francisco had always thought a bit arrogant said, "But they are a lazy lot, these Tiguas, and without ambition. We may have to push them along."

Francisco replied firmly, "No. It is better that we shiver a little."

Fray Juan de Padilla added, "They seem lazy to us only because we are used to judging a man by the success and honors he wins. These mean nothing to the Indians. They do not care for glory or wealth. They try only to live in harmony with the seasons, taking from nature no more than they need. Speak to them with Christian kindness, and they will understand you."

With this advice, the collections progressed smoothly except at Arenal. Three braves of that pueblo came to the general to protest. "We gave all the blankets we could spare," they told him with offended dignity. "We took them from our own shoulders because we felt sorry for your people. But one soldier coveted a blanket worn by a woman of our village. He ran after her, grabbed the blanket roughly, and left her injured and frightened. We do not like it."

"Nor do I," the general assured them. "Come. We will find the man, and he shall be punished."

Although they looked through all the rooms of Alcanfor, the Indians could not identify the selfish villain, nor would his fellow Spaniards tell who it was.

The three warriors went away, muttering their resentment. Coronado had a feeling that trouble would come of it. He noticed that the Tiguas who came every day to barter were less friendly than before. They rolled their eyes in uneasy suspicion. And he didn't like the way they hung around the corrals. They stared at the horses as if fascinated, jumping if anyone spoke to them.

On a crystal and gold morning in December, Coronado was trying to forget his cares over a pleasant breakfast with Fray Juan de Padilla, Captain Cardenas, and Captain Alvarado. Alvarado was describing for them the humpbacked cattle he had seen on the plains.

"They are monstrous beasts!" he declared. "Huge, with great shaggy heads. Their eyes bulge out at the sides, so that when they run they can see anyone who follows them. They are bearded, like goats, and when they run, they carry their heads low so those beards touch the ground. From the belly forward they have thick hair like the mane of a wild lion. Behind, it is fine and woolly like that of a sheep. They have humps larger than a camel's. They have short tails with a bunch of hair on the end. When they run, they carry their tails erect, like a — like a scorpion."

Francisco guffawed. "I can see them exactly! A mixture, I am to understand, Don Hernando, of a goat, a lion, a sheep, a camel, and a scorpion."

The others burst into laughter, too, but Alvarado was too intent to do more than smile. "But huge, Don Francisco."

In the middle of their gay talk the sudden scream and nicker of horses and the pounding of runaway hoofs came as a shock. The general and his guests dashed for the door, upsetting their stools. They joined others running toward the pastures.

There were no horses to be seen! Tracks in the snow pointed north along the river bank; but already the animals were out of sight. Francisco saw a Mexican Indian horseguard bending over a companion on the ground. Blood was running down his back. Father Padilla lifted him to his feet, then stooped to feel the man on the ground. "He is dead," the friar said.

"The Tiguas!" the wounded Mexican gasped. "Their arrows took us by surprise. They have run off with the horses!"

Francisco turned to look for Captain Cardenas. Already the army-master was giving orders to round up the horses which had not been in the pasture. "The others must be recovered at all costs," he said grimly. Soon he and seven or eight armed riders were galloping over the snow, following the tracks along the river. By sundown they were back, with about half the stolen animals and a story that chilled the general's blood.

"We counted more than twenty-five dead horses," Cardenas reported, clipping his words with anger. "At Arenal a palisade of tree trunks has been built around the pueblo, as if for war. Inside, the savages are chasing our horses round and round, shooting arrows to make them run, treating them with every manner of cruelty. One warrior spoke to me, after popping his head over the palisade. I promised there would be no punishment if they returned the horses and acted peacefully."

Francisco nodded approval. "And then?"

"Some others joined him to shout insults at us. They must be punished now, Don Francisco, as a warning to the other towns, or we are lost."

"Without our horses we are indeed lost," Francisco answered.

The general called a council of war, with all the captains and the friars present. They chose about sixty of the best men to return to Arenal with Captain Cardenas. Francisco wanted to go, but Fray Juan de Padilla persuaded him it would be better if he did not take part. But all the next day he walked back and forth, back and forth, in his narrow room, waiting for their return, wishing he were a captain instead of the captain-general.

His first news was brought by a courier on a sweat-

ing horse. "There is furious fighting!" were the quick words. "Captain Cardenas tried for two hours to talk some sense into those Indians. When they waved the tails of our dead horses at us, we gave the *Santiago* and fell upon them. By dark we had gained the first terraces. There we waited till dawn, not daring to sleep. Fighting broke out again at daybreak. Captain Cardenas was everywhere, slashing, pounding, shouting orders! But we can't drive them from their inner rooms. Many of our men are wounded. The captain asks, shall he continue the siege?"

"Hasten back to Arenal on a fresh horse and tell Captain Cardenas to continue the siege. I will bring reinforcements."

Every horse left at Alcanfor was quickly rounded up and saddled. Riding his own big chestnut, the general led his men north through a glittering world of bright sun and crusted snow. Foot soldiers followed after them at their fastest pace.

Francisco felt his ears and nose prickle with cold, but he gulped in the sparkling air gratefully. Before long, however, he smelled an acrid tang.

"Smoke?" Captain Tovar asked him.

Francisco nodded. Soon they could see dark billows of it against the horizon. They dug in their spurs to urge the horses to a swifter gallop.

Before they reached Arenal, they were met by some returning soldiers. "The battle is over. We have taken the pueblo," a young captain reported.

Francisco looked over the fighters. For victors, he thought, they were strangely downcast. It was more than their torn and bloody clothing. Their expressions were troubled. The answers they gave to his questions were confused and vague. But he got from them the disturbing news that some Indians had been burned.

One man told him that some Indians had surrendered under the sign of peace, the symbol of the cross.

Then they had been tied to stakes and burned. He said Captain Cardenas had given the order for the burning.

The heartsick commander understood then what troubled the soldiers. The burning was bad, but even worse to the Spanish sense of honor was the violation of the sign of the cross.

As soon as he found Captain Cardenas, Francisco questioned him sharply.

"The fires were built to light the firebrands used to burn the houses," Cardenas explained as best he could under his own distress. "But I never gave orders that Indians should be burned in them. Nor did I know that any of the natives had surrendered under a sign of peace. It all happened in the heat and excitement of battle. I assure you, Don Francisco, it was not planned that way."

The general's spirit was too bleak to find words of comfort. "Nevertheless, it is a tragedy for all of us."

Pedro de Tovar was more blunt. "Our word of honor will never again be trusted by the Tiguas. And all of us shall have to answer for this day when we return to New Spain."

As if nature itself rebelled against the blackened ruins of Arenal, a fresh white snow began to fall to cover them. Through the blowing drifts of it, the heavyhearted Spaniards rode back to Alcanfor.

9

The Children of Moho

The next day brought a sight which lifted hearts at Alcanfor. It was the rest of the army from Hawikuh, appearing suddenly out of the blank white world to the west. No one was happier to see them and Captain Arellano than Coronado. He had need of the wisdom of the veteran officer.

The new arrivals showed the strain of a hard march. For ten days they had been penned against the walls of a pueblo by a howling blizzard. After that, on the road, they had to clear away the snow every night to make camp. Fortunately the snow was light and dry. It covered them while they slept, keeping them warm. During the day, however, it covered the trail and made the going more difficult.

The welcome at Alcanfor by their old companions warmed their spirits and bodies. The story of the Turk and Quivira fired them with fresh hope which even the tragedy of Arenal and the sight of Bigotes in chains did not dampen.

The general and Captain Arellano got down quickly to practical planning. Coronado said, "Misunderstanding grows like a rolling snowball which threatens to bury all of us. Captain Cardenas went too far at Arenal for us to undo it. When the Turk takes us eastward in the spring, we dare not leave the natives here in rebellion. Every day my scouts bring word that people of the other pueblos are gathering in Moho. Under Juan Aleman's direction, they are fortifying that town with palisades."

With Arellano's approval, the general sent a small detachment to warn Moho: submit and be pardoned, or expect the fate of Arenal.

They came back with word that the Tiguas laughed at them.

Then Captain Cardenas was sent with a larger group to try for peace. The army-master returned with an arrow wound in his leg. "And alive only by the grace of God," he told the council gathered to hear him. "At Moho," he related, "four of us rode up to the wall. I told Juan Aleman that if his people would be friendly, we would treat them well. He seemed pleased, and asked that he and I meet and embrace. He walked out to meet me. I dismounted and put down my arms as my three companions withdrew.

"It was a trick, *señores!* He held me in that embrace while his men rushed up and beat me over the head. Thank the saints my helmet was good Spanish steel! They picked me up to carry me inside the village." The captain's brown eyes flashed as he raised his fist. "I fooled them! The doorway in the palisade is narrow. I braced myself against its sides so they couldn't move me. My friends rescued me there, though several were wounded by stones from the terraces."

Coronado spoke slowly, knowing the risk before them. They were such a small handful in this vast land of savages! "Unless we teach this Juan Aleman respect for the army of Spain, none of us will ever be safe here. Let us march to Moho."

Cheers greeted the bold statement. This time the general took command himself. He wanted no more worried waiting. The whole army set out from Alcanfor, carrying ladders they had made. Grim and determined, they plowed steadily onward through deep snow.

When they reached the charred ruins of Arenal, Coronado led Captain Arellano around the town to point out how the Indians had defended themselves until burned out. "I want no fire at Moho," he stated. "We shall depend on our ladders."

Their approach to the fortified pueblo sent all the Tigua scouts and wood gatherers scurrying to safety inside the walls. Coronado refused to give orders to fire on them. He wanted to make a try for peace himself. While his men fidgeted, he cupped both hands to his mouth and shouted, "Surrender and be unharmed! Let us live in peace."

The Tiguas replied by flinging bits of dead horses over the wall.

At that insult, Coronado drew his sword and thrust it skyward. At the moment of its downswing the Spaniards shouted their *Santiago,* "St. James and at them!" and the battle was on.

Horsemen sought to protect the foot squads running with ladders. Met by a barrage of stones and arrows, they drew back to re-form and try again. Once more, and yet again, they tried to reach the walls. More and more of the Spaniards were felled. These Tiguas were fiercer warriors than the Zuñis of Hawikuh. Even before the early dark came, Coronado signaled a halt.

"Erect our tents to encircle the town," he ordered. "Send all the captains to me."

When the officers were assembled, he told them, "This fighting is too costly. In one day we have lost five dead and sixty wounded. We will do better to lay siege to the town. Food they may have, but their water will soon give out. We shall wait for that."

The waiting called for great courage on both sides. For days and weeks the Spaniards huddled close to the campfires, thinking of their warmer rooms at Alcanfor. The Tiguas were patient within their walls. Just as the besiegers felt sure the Indians must surrender or die of thirst, snow came again, giving the village all the water it needed. Time dragged on until the middle of March. The snows were gone by then, and the water in Moho was gone.

Then Juan Aleman sent out a messenger with a flag of truce, asking for a parley. Francisco decided to talk with the chieftain himself. They met in the open space between the pueblo and the encircling tents. Francisco was shocked at the changed appearance of the Indian. He was gaunt and hollow-cheeked. He wore none of his shell and turquoise ornaments. The flashing pride in the dark eyes had given way to suffering. But the dignity was still there. He did not plead.

Solemnly he said to the general, "We have been told, and we have seen it to be true, that the white strangers do not harm children. Will you let us send ours out to you before they die?"

Coronado had not expected this request. He took time to think. If he agreed, it would mean the warriors could hold out longer. But the thought of suffering children touched him. "Yes," he replied, "we will take care of them."

He chose Lope de Urrea, the gentlest of his captains, to ride up to the barred gate. Urrea went alone and unarmed, without armor or helmet. Francisco held his breath, hoping this was not another trick of Juan Aleman's. He cast a quick glance at his own men near him. Every hand was on a sword hilt, every spur ready to dig in.

Captain Urrea stood in his saddle to reach the top of the wall. A small, big-eyed boy, shivering with fear but making no sound, was placed in his arms. Seating himself in the saddle again, the gentle captain turned and took the boy back to the army. Francisco was pleased to see his tough men trying to quiet the boy's fears. They had water and food ready to give him.

Lope de Urrea rode back to the wall and received a little girl. Back and forth he rode, time after time, until

he was told there were no more children in Moho. Francisco tried to imprint on his memory every part of the scene. It would be a tale to please Doña Beatrice.

Before Captain Urrea left the wall the last time, he again asked the Tiguas to surrender. "You shall be treated as your children have been," he promised.

"We do not believe you!" the Indians shouted, and cries of "Arenal!" rose from the town. A big warrior sprang to the top of the wall, drew back his bowstring, and placed an arrow squarely between the forefeet of Urrea's horse.

As soon as the young officer had calmed his beast, he turned back to join his company. Francisco led the cheers which greeted him.

While the tedious waiting continued, the Spaniards took good care of the children, nearly a hundred of them. Every day the general summoned the Tiguas to make peace, and every day they refused. Then the impatient soldiers tried using battering rams of huge tree trunks against the wall, but it resisted all their efforts. Several of the captains urged the general to let them set fire to the palisade. His answer remained a firm "No."

Then one morning during the fourth watch, that drowsy time just before dawn, Coronado was wakened by an excited messenger. "The Tiguas are escaping from the pueblo," he panted. "They have killed two of our sentinels!"

"Sound the rally," Francisco told him even as he pulled on his clothes. When the bugle call woke the entire camp, the general was ready to lead his men after the Indians. Most of them were captured as they ran for the Rio Grande. Although the river was flooded from the spring's melting snows, other Indians plunged into its icy waters and reached the other bank.

As soon as daylight came, the Spaniards crossed the frothing stream after them. The Tiguas were too weak from cold, starvation, exhaustion, and wounds to put up a fight. They surrendered.

The general gave orders. "Feed them, treat their wounds, but hold them as prisoners of war."

It was the end of March when the army returned to Alcanfor. Francisco was gloomy over the events of the winter. He prayed for better days with the coming of spring.

And with the spring, the Turk's tales of the marvels of Quivira blossomed like the wild flowers in the swales. Now, too, he began to talk more of Harahey, his own province, which lay beyond Quivira. The stories he told of a great chieftain called Tatarrax caused many Spaniards to nod sagely and murmur, "Another Montezuma! We shall surely find another Mexico!"

A few shook their heads as wisely and said, "That Turk is a witchdoctor. He talks with the devil. Believe him not."

But Coronado was one who believed him. He questioned the prisoner at length. "What does he look like, this Lord Tatarrax?" As the Turk replied, he could picture the chieftain: bearded and gray-haired. "Is he fair of face?"

"Yes," the Turk answered. "Furthermore, he prays as the Spaniards do, from a book of hours, and worships a woman whom he calls the Queen of Heaven."

Coronado jumped up and sought Father Padilla. "This Lord Tatarrax is no Indian! He must be a European, perhaps one lost from Cabeza de Vaca's expedition!"

Fray Juan echoed the general's excitement. They must find this lord as soon as they could!

Coronado's first step toward the journey was to restore friendly relations with Pecos, the village of Bigotes and Cacique, which lay on their route eastward. He himself, with Fray Juan and gallant Lope de Urrea, took the old governor home, and promised to bring Bigotes when they came through on their way to Quivira.

The village of Sia, which had given the Spaniards food and clothing during the siege of Moho, and the Keresan pueblos north of Tiguex, were visited and left in a friendly mood. But none of the people of Tiguex would return to their abandoned towns.

While he was getting his gear ready for the eastward journey, Coronado was happier than he had been in months. He liked the singing he heard in camp and the lusty shouts of the soldiers at their work. Now that the gloomy winter was over, spring and adventure beckoned.

112

10

Alvarado's Suspicions

Before Coronado could take his men out of Alcanfor, he had news from the south. Two soldiers rode up from the halfway camp at Corazones which had been under the command of Melchior Diaz. "There is a storm of trouble there," the haggard travelers told the general. "It was bad enough that Captain Diaz died. Then that black-hearted Alcaraz took command. He has made the natives turn against us, and our own men have mutinied."

Francisco scarcely heard the last words. "Did you say Diaz was dead?" he asked. "How did he die?"

"Looking for the ships, Your Grace. We were with him and saw it all." It was late in September, they told him, when they had gone toward the northwest over a barren road, now called the Devil's Highway. It took them to the Colorado River — and word of the ships!

The giant Yuma Indians were still full of wonder and talk about the great canoes with sails which had appeared on their river farther south. For three days the Diaz party hurried down the stream they called the Firebrand, because of the Yumas' habit of carrying torches to keep themselves warm.

They were too late; the ships had gone. Diaz found only a note carved on a tree trunk: "Alarcon came this far. There are letters at the foot of this tree."

From the letters Diaz learned that the ships had come as far up the river as they could and then, unable to get any news of the army, had sailed back to New Spain. On their journey they had discovered that Lower California was not an island as Cortéz had thought, but a peninsula.

On a day not long after, Diaz was exploring the shoreline of the Gulf of California when he saw his greyhound chasing some sheep they had brought along. Meaning to frighten the dog, he galloped forward and threw his lance. It struck the ground in front of his horse. The horse shied, and Diaz slipped and fell squarely upon the quivering shaft.

114

The astonished soldiers thought him dead. To their amazement he roused and doctored himself. Inspired by his dauntless spirit, they put him on a litter and started back to Corazones as fast as they could go. But on the twentieth day, Melchior Diaz died. His grieving men buried him on a hillside in the wilderness and marked the grave with a cross.

Coronado sighed and said, "No braver, better, or more gallant man ever lived."

Then he went off by himself to think over the problem of Corazones. Since they must return to New Spain that way, through the Sonora Valley, it was important that those Indians be friendly. He had counted on taking all his men to Quivira, where he might have need of every sword and bow. He knew, too, that every man wanted to go with him. Nevertheless, he must send a force back to Sonora to settle the disturbance there. He selected Pedro de Tovar to be commander on this dangerous mission.

To soften the disappointment of these men, Coronado told them, "As soon as the trouble is settled, Captain Tovar will bring you back to Tiguex to follow our trail to Quivira. I will leave crosses along the way to guide you."

Riding south beside Captain Tovar were couriers

with letters to the king, the viceroy, Doña Beatrice, and the soldiers' families.

With Sonora thus attended to, Coronado turned his thoughts again to Quivira. On April 23, he held a review of the forces at Alcanfor. As he watched the men file by, he thought of the difference between this and the brilliant review at Compostela little more than a year ago. The men were shaggy-haired now, their armor rusty, clothes tattered, and banners frayed. But they still had enough horses, cattle, and sheep. They still had their Indian allies, with the captives of Moho in addition.

Instead of Fray Marcos to guide them to Cibola, they had the Turk to lead them to Quivira. They still had hope, determination and courage, and provisions for thirty days. They had even more affection and admiration for their young commander. They had a better spirit of working together, and more experience of the trail. There would be no lost packsaddles on this journey.

The Turk protested against their taking provisions. "You will tire the horses. They should be fresh to bring back the gold. Food will be plentiful all along the way."

Nevertheless, the quest began with loaded pack-horses and the cattle and sheep in the procession which set out from Alcanfor in the quickening springtime. The soldier whose duty it was to count the steps in each day's march called, "One, two, three, four . . ." and the search was on.

The explorers crossed the Rio Grande, their River of Our Lady, and jogged north along its greening banks. They skirted the Sandia Mountains and turned eastward. They passed the big turquoise mines in the Galisteo Valley, and from there probably crossed through Glorieta Pass.

On the fourth day they came to Pecos, the most eastern and the strongest of the pueblos. It rose, four stories high, around a square plaza, with a parapet around the second story making it a real fortress. Coronado looked it over, hoping he would never have to do battle here.

It was with a strong feeling of relief that he handed Bigotes back to his townsmen. It had hurt him to keep the big chieftain a captive. But all this time the proud Indian had remained too stubborn to tell the whereabouts of the golden bracelet.

To show their pleasure over Bigotes' return, the elders of Pecos gave Coronado another captive from Quivira, a boy named Zabe. He was a stolid, dark lad who disliked talking. He answered the general's questions with grunts. Since he didn't seem very helpful as a guide, he was allowed to walk in the rear with Sopete, rather than in front with the Turk.

As highhearted as the dewy May morning around them, the Spaniards were soon traveling southeast, with the Pecos River on their left. It roared along in full spring flood from the melting snows. They marched for four days before they found a good place to build a bridge across the stream. It was near present Anton Chico. With everyone working and singing and repeating new stories told by the Turk, the bridge was put up in another four days. It shook to the rumble of horses, cattle, sheep, and marching men, but held stoutly.

From the bridge the travelers moved slowly eastward over a desertlike plateau. They passed near present Newkirk, and continued somewhat as Highway 66 runs today. This level country broke off into cliffs, like palisades. Because of these, the Spaniards named it *Llano Estacado,* meaning Palisaded Plains.

Tucumcari Peak became a landmark for them. And then they came to the buffalo, migrating in herds so vast they blocked the horizon from view. Francisco had found it hard to believe that even one such shaggy, great-headed beast existed, and here they were by the thousands! Day after day the world was full of them from rim to rim, from dawn to dark.

"You remember," Captain Cardenas remarked one afternoon, "that Marco Polo wrote of seeing humpbacked

118

cattle in Asia? Could these be the same, do you think?"

Captain Alvarado slapped his knee. "That he did! I think it likely we might be in Asia, eh, Don Francisco?"

"It is possible, *señores,* but I think not. He mentioned no pueblos, as I remember. Still, it is a part of our duty to find out."

The three friends rode in silence until Tristan de Arellano and Diego Lopez motioned them to ride over to where they were. Captain Arellano pointed to curious marks on the ground. "Dragging lances would leave such tracks," he said. "There must be natives close by."

Coronado sent for the Turk. As soon as that eagle-nosed Indian saw the tracks, he smiled and led them eagerly to a village of tents. The residents, about fifty people, were Querechos, a branch of the Apache tribe. They were not afraid. They stood in the openings of their painted, buffalo-hide teepees and stared at the strangers.

The Turk conversed with them easily, for he knew their language. When the other captains came up, the Indians changed to sign language to answer their questions about Quivira. Their fluent hands made the sign of a large river toward the rising sun. Villages were thick along its course. After reaching Haxa, the first one, they could travel ninety days without leaving settlements. There were large canoes on the river. A bearded man was lord of that kingdom.

Coronado was jubilant. "It is just as the Turk has told us!"

But Captain Alvarado was disturbed. He bit his lip and frowned. "Something puzzles me, Don Francisco. It was near this same place last autumn that the Turk wanted me to go on to Quivira by turning north. It was here he told me about the bracelet. As soon as I heard that, of course, I turned back to hasten to you with the story. Now why do these Indians tell us to go east?"

Francisco turned to the Turk. "They are right," the Indian assured him. "We must go east. Not north."

Alvarado excused himself and rode away. In a little while he returned and took the general off to one side. "I have talked to the tattooed Indian, Sopete. He says his country, Quivira, is north, as the Turk told us last year."

Coronado shrugged. "Oh, don't listen to Sopete, Don Hernando. He has a grudge against the Turk and will say anything to dispute him. After all, what reason would the Turk have for deceiving us?"

Next day the Apaches moved their camp. Francisco watched with amazement as they quickly took down their teepees and harnessed one end of the long tent poles to dogs. The folded tent and other possessions were then strapped to the poles. The dogs pulled these over the ground, leaving the marks which Arellano had found.

The Spaniards moved on also, going along the valley of the Canadian River. In two days they found another Querecho tent village. Here, as before, the Turk explained to the Indians who the bearded, pale-skinned strangers were; then Coronado asked them questions.

They told him, to his joy, "There are rich settlements along the big river toward the rising sun."

"See, the Turk was right," Francisco said to Alvarado.

But the young captain was not convinced. "Let us test him," he suggested. "He says Haxa, the first settlement, is now but two days east of here and has an abundance of maize. If you were to send a scouting party ahead to barter for some, and keep the Turk here . . ."

Coronado agreed. "I will send Captain Cardenas."

In the early freshness of the following morning, Francisco was standing beside the lean army-master while his men got their horses and pack mules ready. "If this turns out as the Turk says," Francisco confided, "Don Hernando will feel better about following the Turk's directions."

Captain Cardenas had to quiet his skittish horse before he could reply. "Pay no attention to Don Hernando and Sopete. After all, these Indians agree with the Turk. They ought to know."

He put his foot in the stirrup. At that moment a commotion broke out among some Querechos not far away. The startled horse jumped and reared. His hoofs slipped, and he fell with a loud thump, knocking the breath out of him and throwing Cardenas to the ground. One arm lay twisted beneath the heavy saddle.

"Bring the surgeon!" Francisco grunted as he hauled at the stunned horse to release his friend.

The doctor came on the run. While he set the broken arm, Francisco suffered with the pale captain, gritting his teeth against the crunching of the bones. Then he helped carry Cardenas to his tent.

As soon as he was breathing easier, Francisco teased him. "Ho, now, friend Garcia, a fine trick to play on me. How am I to get along with a one-armed army-master?"

"You can't," Cardenas replied in his always serious manner. "You must appoint another."

Francisco named the steadfast Diego Lopez, a stocky *hidalgo* who had earned the trust of everyone in the expedition. "Your first task," the general told him, "is to make the trip to Haxa. Go with all speed. I shall expect you back in four days." He gave Captain Lopez his sea-compass to use for guide. This was a magnetized needle hung on a silken thread.

The army settled down to await the return of the scouting party. The men were pleased, as it would give them a chance to go buffalo hunting, a sport they were eager to try under the teaching of the friendly Querechos.

And the general hoped to have an exciting report from Diego Lopez. Haxa, he hoped, might have more than corn that was yellow.

11

The
Hard
Truth

On their first day of waiting in the Querecho village, most of the Spaniards went out with the Indian hunters to learn how they brought down the lumbering buffalo. It was always amazing how the Indians could single out a great bull and, having separated him from the herd, drive a spear or arrow into his heart.

The hunters returned in the evening, tired but excited, each man happy or disgruntled according to his success or lack of it. One small group, however, immediately sought the general. They were in distress because one of their men was missing. "We shouted and searched

124

and left bone markers," they said, "but we were not able to find him nor he us."

Francisco acted at once. He knew the panic a man must feel, lost in this flat, unmarked country. He set the trumpeters to riding around the camp making all the noise they could. He had beacon fires built of dry grass and buffalo chips. He stayed up all night to see they were kept burning. But the lost hunter did not return.

Four anxious days passed, and another and another, and he was not found. His friends gave up hope and mourned him as dead. The Indians said it was not possible he could still be alive.

Six days had passed, and Diego Lopez and his scouts had not returned from Haxa. Were they lost, too? Francisco thought with a shudder how easily this country could swallow up the whole expedition. His relief was immense when Captain Lopez and his men trotted into camp, safe and well.

"No, we were not lost," the new army-master told the troubled general, "but Haxa is. I followed the sea-compass an extra day to the east, and saw nothing but cattle and sky, and more cattle and sky. There were no settlements of any kind."

"Hola!" Francisco said. "Here is a new worry. Hernando de Alvarado will be sure to claim the Turk has lied. But there must be some explanation." He sent for the Indian. Watching him carefully, he had the army-master repeat his statements.

The Turk was not embarassed. He only shrugged and said, "Perhaps I made a little mistake in the distance, and Haxa is still farther east. In this land . . . distances . . . " He shrugged again and smiled slyly. "Or perhaps the compass is not as good a guide as I am."

Francisco looked at the Indian a long time. His words were reasonable. Surely he was telling the truth! Francisco was sorry he had mistrusted him.

So for five days Coronado's men followed the Turk and the pointing fingers of the Querechos toward the rising sun, again going along the valley of the Canadian River. They crossed the meridian which later would separate New Mexico and Texas. Then they left the valley and climbed to the high, flat plains around Vega, in the Texas Panhandle.

Francisco thought he had seen flat land before, but this region was as smooth and endless as the sea. His army left no more trace on it than a ship does on the ocean, for the grass rose up again after it was trampled. Since he could find no wood for the crosses to mark the way for Pedro de Tovar and the men who had gone to Corazones, he left piles of rocks and sun-bleached bones.

The army moved across the plains merrily enough, the men marveling at many things: the vastness of the flat land, the heat of the sun during the burning days, and the splendor of the stars at night.

The horses were better off than the men here, for they cropped the finest pasture land on the continent. The sweet buffalo grass stretched for hundreds of miles. By this time the corn for the men was used up. Like the Apaches, they were living on nothing but meat — their own cattle and the buffalo they killed.

They saw more and more of the Arablike Apaches. "They are more numerous than the pueblo people, it seems to me," Fray Juan de Padilla remarked one day.

"Yes," Captain Arellano agreed, "and they are of finer figure."

"But they don't have the arts of weaving and pottery like the people of Cibola and Tiguex," said Diego Lopez.

"That is because they must follow the buffalo," Fray Juan replied. "It is amazing the way they live off the beasts. They need nothing else except their pack dogs. They have the flesh for food, the blood for drink, the skin for tents and clothing. I have seen them make awls and thread from the bones and sinews. The dried chips are their only fuel. I have even seen them use the stomachs for carrying water. As long as they have the bison,

127

the Apaches will have a good living," said the friar.

Francisco only half listened. He missed Captain Cardenas, who was riding in the rear on a gentle mule led by foot-soldiers. And he was disturbed by the attitude of Alvarado. The eager captain who used to ride ahead of everyone now kept himself in the rear with Sopete and the Indians, as if the sight of the Turk upset him.

And Francisco had to admit that he himself was baffled by the eagle-beaked guide. They had been traveling for almost three weeks since leaving the Querecho villages, and still had not found Haxa! The Turk kept saying it was just ahead, always a little farther on. And the Querechos still agreed with him.

One evening, after their guides had turned them gradually southward, Alvarado exploded angrily. The army was making camp for the night. He and the general were walking a little apart, their long shadows leaping from the light of the fires. "I tell you, Don Francisco, Sopete has convinced me that we are going in the wrong direction! We are going away from Quivira!"

Coronado strode back and forth, his face puckered, his eyes showing his distress. "But why shouldn't the Turk want us to go to Quivira? And why do the Querechos agree with him?"

"Sopete says the Turk gets them to tell you whatever he wants them to. If you'll remember, he always talks to them before we do, in a strange language."

Francisco nodded, biting his thumbnail. Alvarado was right. "What we must do, then," he said, "is question some natives before he sees them."

The next Indians they found were of a different tribe. They called themselves Teyas. They were camped in a ravine unlike any other than Francisco had seen. This was a rough gash in the earth at the eastern end of the *Llano Estacado*, where it drops away to lower prairies. It was probably what is now called Tule Canyon. The Teyas welcomed the Spaniards as the Querechos had done: without fear, but with amazement at their horses.

Coronado quickly asked them about Quivira.

"Quivira! It is the other way!" they said, pointing north.

Then they told him that the Quivirans were not rich. They had houses of grass, not of stone or adobe or even skins.

Coronado groaned. "Bring Sopete to me," he asked Fray Juan. The friar returned in short order with the slave and Captain Alvarado. Sopete's black eyes were flashing in their tattooed circles.

"He's been furiously angry," Alvarado explained, "vowing to kill the Turk and the Querechos and most of us."

The Indian spluttered a mixture of Spanish and his native tongue and flailed the air with his hands in sign language. Francisco understood him perfectly. He wanted to go home, to Quivira, and they were not going the right way. And no one would believe him!

"I do now, Sopete," Coronado admitted. "Don Hernando, will you fetch the Turk and Zabe?"

The two Indians, the eagle-beaked one and the silent boy, were soon brought. Looks of hatred flashed between Sopete and the Turk. They both wanted to talk at once.

Francisco demanded silence. He turned to Zabe. "Which way lies Quivira?"

Zabe pointed north.

"Why did the Querechos lead us southeast, then?"

Zabe pointed to the Turk.

"Does he speak the truth?" Francisco demanded of the skinny Turk. The Indian only shrugged and glared at Zabe spitefully. But Coronado, feeling sick inside, knew at last that he had been deceived. This man whom he had trusted, whose talk he had so enjoyed . . . "Why did you do it?" he asked.

Another shrug was the only answer. But the expression of gloating triumph on the Turk's face made Francisco want to strike him. He raised his hands. Then he dropped them. Anger would do no good. It was too late for that.

He asked Sopete, "Will you guide us to Quivira?"

"Yes, if you will give me my freedom and let me

stay there. And if you keep him out of my sight!" He spat toward the Turk.

Coronado promised, then turned to Alvarado. "Don Hernando, keep the Turk under careful guard. And keep him hidden!"

That taken care of, the general called a council of his captains and the friars. Plans had to be changed, and quickly. "The business of Fray Marcos and Cibola was not of my doing," Coronado told his officers earnestly, "but this following of the Turk I myself and no one else brought upon us."

Arellano protested. "No. We were all to blame. We all believed him except Don Hernando."

"Thank you, Don Tristan," Francisco said, with some relief. "But now, because we are so far off our trail and are short of food and water, and mostly because the Turk was probably lying about the riches to be found in Quivira, it is my opinion that the main part of the army should return to Tiguex. I will take thirty men on our fastest horses and see what is in the kingdom of Quivira."

Not one man objected to the plan. But as usual, neither did they wish to be in the party returning to Tiguex. They wanted to go with the general.

"We will go together to a better camp site the Teyas

132

have told me about," Coronado said, "and make our final plans there."

While they were getting ready to leave, a tattooed Indian woman, a Quiviran who had been a slave at Moho and was now, with her captors, a slave to the Spaniards, escaped from the camp.

"Should we send Sopete after her, Your Grace?" Francisco was asked.

But Sopete said, "Please, let her go free. She knows this country. She will not be lost."

The general agreed. "What difference can a runaway squaw make to us?"

A few years later, the men with Coronado were glad that they had not gone after her. This nameless woman of the Wichitas will have a place forever in the history of our country because she linked together two great exploring expeditions. Because of her, the width of the North American continent could be estimated for the first time.

Slightly more than a year after she ran away from Coronado's army in the ravines of west Texas, she met other Spaniards in what is now east Texas. They were the survivors of Hernando de Soto's expedition, which had landed in Florida and discovered the Mississippi River on its way westward.

She told De Soto's men that the ravines where she escaped from Spaniards like themselves were nine days' travel from their encampment. Ragged and hungry, they did not try to find the ravines, but turned south to the Gulf, where they made boats which took them to the coast of New Spain.

Throughout the colony their story of the tattooed woman was heard and retold with interest and amazement. In time it reached Europe and the mapmakers.

The explorers moved northward as May of 1541 was giving way to June. They made an outlandish parade through the Texas Panhandle country. Sun-blistered, rough-haired men in odd combinations of European and Indian clothing either walked or rode bay, black, or chestnut horses. At their head, the gold-helmeted general was flanked by Sopete and Zabe. Fray Juan de Padilla in his patched robe moved tirelessly up and down the line. Behind the soldiers were the Mexican Indians in all the tribal costumes of New Spain. Last came the slow herds of cattle, sheep, and extra horses.

In front, on the sides, and all around the procession, moved the Teyas, friendly and curious. They were intelligent people, modestly dressed in tanned hides and in blankets they got by trade from the pueblos. They traveled with the parade until it reached the last village in their territory. For all their friendliness, the Spaniards found it easier to journey without such a mob. Only a few stayed with them to guide them to the good camping place.

This was in a deep canyon with a wide valley. Beside the meadow-bordered stream were grapevines, wild roses, nut and mulberry trees. The walls of the chasm, with their wind-carved battlements of red, yellow, and purple, brought words of awe. Only those who had seen the Grand Canyon of Arizona had seen anything more spectacular than this Palo Duro Canyon cut through the *Llano Estacado* by the Prairie Dog fork of the Red River.

Here Coronado called in the soldiers who had been counting their steps. He figured they had come six hundred and fifty miles in the thirty-seven days since they had left Tiguex.

12

Lord Tatarrax
and the
Turk

When everyone was com-
fortably settled and the men
were busy sun-drying strips
of meat as the Indians had
taught them, the general called another council of his
officers. Captain Tristan de Arellano, who had done so
well at trailing the cattle on their other journeys, was
placed in command of the group returning to Tiguex. It
was thought best that Captain Cardenas return with
them, because of his broken arm. Zabe offered to guide
them back a shorter way.

Among the thirty going to Quivira were Diego
Lopez, the army-master, and Captain Alvarado. Fray
Juan de Padilla refused to be left behind. The Turk, once

more in chains, was kept in the rear where Sopete would not have to look at him.

Coronado returned to the high plains west of the canyons to make his march, carefully following his sea-compass northward. His Teya guides had another system for staying on course. They would check where the sun rose and shoot an arrow in the direction they wished to take. Before coming to it, they would shoot another over it, then another and another, until they reached the place where they planned to spend the night.

Coronado and his men had journeyed almost a week when two couriers from the main army overtook them.

"What could have happened back there?" he asked with a quick frown as he ripped into the paper they gave him. After a hurried reading, he laughed and passed the letter on to Diego Lopez. To the others he explained, "It is a petition from the men, begging to be allowed to go with us, even yet."

To the couriers he said, "Tell the men that their spirit pleases me, but that what they ask would not be wise, as we all agreed. However, if we find anything of value, it shall be divided equally among all of us."

Coronado's fast force moved northward with the migrating bison for nearly thirty days, living on buffalo meat all the way. They rode across the Texas and Oklahoma panhandles, then took a slight swing eastward through what is now southern Kansas.

Francisco was happier than he had yet been on the whole journey. At last he was leading an exploration himself. While he had little hope of finding another Aztec-land, there was still a chance that some treasure might be found. And he clung to the belief that the Lord Tatarrax might be a Christian, even a Spaniard. The happiest feeling of all was that after seeing Quivira, they could go home.

On June 29 they came to a large river, green and smooth-flowing. Sopete danced with pleasure when they stopped on its low bank and the Spaniards dismounted to drink of its refreshing waters. "We are almost at my home!" he exclaimed, with joy replacing the sullen anger in his black eyes. "This is the river of Quivira." He pointed a finger along its eastward-running course. "The villages are only a few days away."

Coronado felt his own excitement mounting. He sprang to his horse, put spurs to flank, and splashed across the ford on sand packed hard by thousands of bison hoofs. Years later the Santa Fe Trail would cross the Arkansas River at this same spot near Ford, Kansas.

Fray Juan de Padilla was excited too. "What a beautiful, green country! Something in it calls to me, something, maybe, that reminds me of my old home."

Three days after crossing the river, the Spaniards saw their first Quivirans, a hunting party. Francisco caught only a brief glimpse of them, for at first sight of the strangers on horseback, they gave terrified shrieks and fled.

"Go after them, Sopete," the general called, holding his own men back. In a little while Sopete returned with his fellow-tribesmen, their fright turned into curiosity. Coronado exchanged amused glances with his captains over Sopete's new air of importance. Even the elders of the hunting party stood in awe of him.

As soon as they got over their amazement, the Quivirans welcomed the Spaniards warmly and wanted to show them their whole kingdom. The general promised to explore all of it. "Where lives the Lord Tatarrax?" he asked.

"In the last village," they replied.

"Find me a swift messenger," he told Sopete. Then he dismounted, seated himself on a flat rock, and wrote a letter to the chieftain — in Spanish. After telling briefly of his journey, he offered help if any Europeans were in captivity and wished to escape. A fleet-footed young warrior folded it into his belt and sped away.

The rest of the Wichitas, as the people of Quivira

were later called, led the strangers to their villages, past Pawnee Rock and the Great Bend of the Arkansas and across the tributaries of that river, in the vicinity of present Lyons, Kansas.

There were settlements along the streams, but they were not at all as the Turk had pictured them. There were no trees with golden bells, no golden plates, no gold-prowed canoes. But the maize, plums, and grapes were a delight to the meat-sated Spaniards.

After the ceremony of possession, Diego Lopez said, "At least we have added one more kingdom to the Spanish crown."

"Such as it is," Captain Alvarado added drily. "I doubt whether any Spaniard would ever wish to settle here."

Fray Juan de Padilla spoke up with gusto. "This one would! There is something about this land that I like very much. The green meadows, the charming rivers with their fine waters, these tall, proud people."

For twenty-five days the Wichitas guided the explorers through their land, past many settlements of grass-thatched, round lodges with smoke rising from holes in the roof. The people wore but little clothing in the warm weather. Many were tattooed, like Sopete and the woman who had run away. All were friendly and gave allegiance to the Spanish king with ready cheerfulness.

It was mid-August by the time the Spaniards reached Tabas, the last village of Quivira, on Smoky Hill River. Lindsborg is now not far from the place where they were to meet the mysterious Tatarrax. They set up their camp on the yellowing prairies and waited impatiently for his appearance.

First came a runner to announce the approach of the lordly chieftain. Coronado lined up his men as for review. He could hear them murmuring among themselves as they waited, and their questions echoed his own thoughts. Would Tatarrax be a European? Would he be pleased by their coming or resentful?

A hush fell upon the Spaniards the moment two hundred semi-naked warriors marched into view. They were large men, with feather headdresses atop faces streaked with red, blue, and yellow paint. Many a Spaniard's hand started toward his sword at sight of their lances and bows.

The line of warriors parted. A giant of a man strode forward. His copper skin gleamed beneath his paint and feathers. From a beardless face he stared at the pale-skinned strangers who were staring at him. Coronado grunted with disappointment. Lord Tatarrax was every

inch an Indian! The Turk had lied again.

The chieftain was an elderly man with deep lines adding to the dignity of his face. He expressed, through Sopete as interpreter, the honor and pleasure this meeting brought him. Coronado returned the greeting, then, as soon as it was polite to do so, pointed to a copper ornament at the Indian's throat. "Is this from your kingdom?" he asked hopefully.

Tatarrax had a young brave remove the copper ornament, and he gave it to the general. But he did not give the answer which would have pleased Francisco more. "No," he replied, "it came from lands that are farther on."

So, Francisco thought, there is not even copper in Quivira. When he questioned the Indians about these lands farther on, they made signs indicating settlements like their own. He could see no need to explore farther, but he called his men together to get their opinions.

"What ought we to do?" he asked. "Shall we go on, stay here for the winter, or return to Tiguex?"

Diego Lopez, as army-master, spoke first. "We are such a small group; let us join the rest of the army in Tiguex before winter blocks our way."

Captain Jaramillo added quickly, "When spring comes again, we can come back here with all our forces and go to these lands farther on."

The rest of the thirty men agreed to this plan. Francisco kept to himself his longing to turn homeward, to set out on the trail to the City of Mexico.

Diego Lopez rose to his feet again. "Your Grace, as I have said before, I think we should execute the Turk."

Coronado's eyes glinted as he replied, "And as I have said before, Captain, what honor is to be gained by killing him?"

Diego Lopez answered in a voice hard-held to calmness. "Our men wonder why you protect him. It is a cause of much grumbling."

Captain Zaldivar spoke up quickly. "He has told these people to give us no more maize. He is urging them to kill our horses. He has told them we are devils who will burn them alive."

Several of the captains began talking at once. The buzz of conversation grew louder with excitement. Alvarado almost shouted to make himself heard. "Without doubt he should be executed, Don Francisco!"

Francisco raised a hand for silence. "I would hear what the Turk has to say to these charges. Will you bring him, Captain Lopez?"

The Turk swaggered into the presence of the Spaniards. He met their cold looks with an arrogant laugh. "You will never leave this village!" he shouted at them. "You and those beasts you ride will all be dead. I could not lose you on the plains as I promised the men of Pecos, but you shall die in Quivira. Bigotes will have his revenge!"

Francisco felt shocked at first, then slowly a great anger rose in him as he understood what the Turk was saying. "Bigotes wanted revenge?"

"Yes! He paid me to lead you astray so you would

144

die of hunger. Even the gift of Zabe was for that purpose, only he refused to help me."

With a shiver, remembering the hunter who had never been found, Coronado realized how close to success the Turk had come.

Several of the captains started for the Turk, Alvarado with drawn sword. Even as Coronado was ordering them to hold back, Sopete rushed in. He pointed a finger at the Turk. "He has been trying to stir up my people to kill you. But you will not be harmed in my country," he assured the Spaniards.

The Turk sputtered with anger for a moment, then once more the soldiers heard his arrogant laugh. "By now the rest of your army is dead! The warriors of Pecos were set to kill any who returned."

The general had one more question for the Turk. "Was there ever a golden bracelet?"

The hawk-nosed Indian laughed again. "No. It was a tale I made up."

Coronado at last agreed that one task had to be done before they left Tabas. Quietly, in the tent shared by Diego Lopez and Juan de Zaldivar, the Turk was choked to death with a rope around his neck.

13

The Hoof
of
Fate

The Spaniards back-tracked
through the grass hut villages of Quivira on double
marches, not bothering to
pitch their tents at night, often going on after dark. They
recrossed the river of Quivira, the Arkansas, at the same
sandy ford. Then they followed their six Quiviran guides
on a straight line to the Querecho village on the Canadian River, avoiding three hundred miles of travel.

It was here, Francisco remembered, that Captain
Cardenas had broken his arm. He wondered what the
next news of Don Garcia might be. If only he had
listened to Captain Alvarado and Sopete when they left
this village on their outward journey! Would his blind-

ness now cost the lives of Arellano and his army? Would they all be captives now, or would he find them dead on a battlefield? In his mind, as they hastened on to Pecos, he made plans for whatever he might find.

They reached the Pecos River and their bridge, still spanning the stream. Now, in the late autumn, there was hardly any water under it. A few more days, and the flat-roofed fortress town was seen on the horizon. Indian fashion, Coronado put his ear to the ground. No sound. Good sign or bad? He didn't know. He signaled his horsemen on.

Soon a swirling dust cloud coming their way resolved itself into a galloping Spaniard. Francisco dug in his spurs and dashed to meet him. It was Captain Urrea, who shouted, "Praise the saints you are safe!"

"And your army?" Coronado called out.

"All safe!"

Francisco let himself sag with relief while the young officer pulled his horse to a rearing stop close to him and said, "I sent word to Captain Arellano as soon as I heard your hoofbeats. I was on sentry duty looking for you."

In almost no time Arellano and about forty men rode up. All the Spaniards slid from their panting mounts and mingled together, with embraces and slappings of shoulders and a great hubbub of talk.

"Did you meet with trouble at Pecos?" Francisco asked Arellano anxiously.

"Yes, we did. Why do you ask?"

When Coronado told him of the Turk's confession, the veteran captain nodded soberly. "So that explains it. The warriors of Bigotes did indeed challenge us to battle. But after we killed two of their braves, they withdrew inside their pueblo. Probably they didn't expect so many of us to return." He chuckled drily. "We went on to Alcanfor to get prepared for the winter, and then I came back here with this small force to prevent your being attacked."

Coronado could laugh now that all was well. "And we were rushing back to help you! Well, Don Tristan, one thing I know: there will be no more splitting of our army. Not as far from home as this. But let us see if we can't make Pecos more friendly before we leave."

The general visited Bigotes, and the natural courtesy of the two men and the mutual liking which had sprung up at their first meeting in Hawikuh offset the later troubles. When the Spaniards left for Alcanfor, Pecos was friendly.

As they rode west together, Arellano assured the general that there was enough food for the winter, which they must spend, once more, in Tiguex. They had plenty of dried buffalo meat. And the captains had been able to barter for corn all the way from the northern town of Taos to the pueblos as far south as present day El Paso.

"The natives were all friendly," Arellano told him, "except the Tiguas. They still hide from us."

The first light flurry of snow began to fall as Coronado was getting settled in Alcanfor. On a day in October, the secretary Bermejo put quills, ink, and parchment on a table in the general's room, and then withdrew. Francisco planned to write to the king and the viceroy about the journey to Quivira.

He sat with quill in hand, considering where to start, when Fray Juan de Padilla came in. He picked up the copper ornament given Francisco by Lord Tatarrax and fingered its design. "I wonder where it was made, and by whom, and how many tradings it has gone through. A curious trinket. You should send it to the viceroy."

"Instead of the gold he expected us to find!"

"Remember this, my son," the friar scolded him, "not even Cortéz can find gold where there is none. And not even that great captain could have directed this expedition any better than you have done."

Francisco shrugged and laughed. "Your words cheer me, Father. But tell me truly, how do the soldiers feel about the expedition?"

"Just as I do. Their only worry is that you will take us home in the spring instead of back to Quivira."

Francisco shook his head. "A strange thing. Even after they have seen the land."

"Well, those who were there think if only we had gone farther . . . And of course those who didn't go think they could find things we missed. It is Zabe's fault, really. He keeps telling them there is gold there, although not as much as the Turk said."

"Zabe wants to lead us back, I think, so he can become as important as Sopete," Coronado replied.

Before he could get back to his writing, Alvarado appeared at his door, breathing hard and looking excited.

"Come in, Don Hernando. You have news?"

"Indeed I do! Pedro de Tovar is here!"

"Here and at your service," Captain Tovar called out, entering the room.

The two men embraced heartily; then questions burst from each at the same time. "Why do we find you here and not in Quivira?" Tovar asked.

"How did you leave things in Corazones?" Coronado had asked in the same breath. He answered first, however, explaining briefly the deceit of the Turk and the disappointment at Quivira.

Captain Tovar said he had found nothing but

trouble in the beautiful Sonora Valley. "It was as bad as was reported to you, Don Francisco. The soldiers had mutinied against Captain Alcaraz. The angry Indians are tipping their arrows with poison. Even a slight wound causes death. I moved the settlement a hundred miles to the north, to Opata country and brought about half the garrison back with me, hoping to follow your crosses to Quivira. But I do have some good news. I have brought letters!"

The letters brought jubilation to Alcanfor. They had been sent by courier to Corazones from Mexico City. Many of the men had news of their families for the first time since leaving New Spain. Francisco closed his door to everyone while he read over and over his messages from Doña Beatrice and Antonio de Mendoza.

Captain Cardenas received word that his older brother in Spain had died, leaving the family estates to him. The viceroy had sent him permission to go home to Spain to attend to his inheritance.

Alvarado teased him. "Do not scorn us, Don Garcia, when you are wealthy and we who looked for wealth are poor."

Since Captain Cardenas wished to leave at once, Coronado entrusted to him the letters for the king and the viceroy, which he had at last completed, and the articles for Mendoza. He told him, "When you have an audience with the king, Don Garcia, assure him we have done our best."

The trouble in Sonora was very much on the general's mind as he bade good-by to Captain Cardenas and his traveling group of a dozen men. "Expect anything in those green valleys," he cautioned. "Post your guards well. Keep alert."

Cardenas' voice was even more serious than usual as he put his uninjured arm around Francisco's shoulder. "You keep alert here, too. Our men are restless and getting bored with this idle life. Keep them busy if you can."

But it was hard, at Alcanfor, for men to stay busy. They took turns herding the ever-decreasing cattle and sheep. They mended gear and cooked their meals. A few made trips to pueblos to trade for clothing. Trade goods were scarce by now, so shields and spears were bartered for blankets and corn. It was expected, however, that Juan Gallego — who had left Hawikuh a year and a half ago to bring supplies from Mexico City — would arrive with his pack-train before the army started east again.

The general talked often with Fray Juan de Padilla, whose vigorous good nature did much to keep things peaceful and to keep the general's spirits raised.

"Cheer up," Fray Juan said to Francisco one day in December. "We have found souls to save. That is the greatest wealth of all. Ah, you are homesick, my friend. And some of your men, too, though none will admit it for fear of being thought fainthearted."

Coronado rose and stretched. "The men grumble so, Fray Juan! These houses are warmer than our tents, but they feel cramped, they say. They complain of favoritism. I've been as fair as I know how."

The Franciscan threw up a hand. "As an old soldier myself, let me tell you that all armies are so when idle. And when you remember that many of your men were spoiled young *hidalgos* when the expedition began . . . Ah, don't worry. You are still the best-loved commander to venture forth in the New World."

"Thank you, Father. You do hearten me. Well, I promised Rodrigo Maldonado a race this afternoon. It will afford some amusement in the camp and exercise for us. Will you come with me?"

The two tall men climbed down the wooden ladder from the general's second-floor room and headed for the corral. Francisco chose a fast sorrel for his racing horse. "Give me a new saddle girth today," he told the groom, "and cinch it tight. I must put this Maldonado in his place. Last time he flew from me as the very wind."

The general was pleased to see his soldiers in a gay mood, to hear their cheers as he trotted to the starting line. All cheered again when Captain Maldonado rode out to join him. It was an old debate among the Spaniards as to which of the two men was the better rider.

The horses strained at their reins, eager to run. Francisco breathed in the cold air, glanced at the shimmering land around him, and felt almost happy. He grinned cockily at the dashing, dark-eyed Maldonado.

Then came the cry of the starter, and they were off! Coronado could feel the stretch of his horse's muscles. He became a part of the rhythm of the running. This was great! He was ahead! He hugged his knees tighter against the sorrel, urging him on.

Suddenly the world gave way. Francisco felt himself flying; then he knew nothing more.

So fast that it happened in the space of a breath, the general was down, his saddleless horse was plunging ahead, and Maldonado, white-faced, was trying to pull his horse to one side. There was not time. The speeding animal hit the general's head with a flying hoof.

The watchers were stunned. There lay their splendid young commander, a crumpled heap on the ground.

Seeing that Coronado still breathed, Fray Juan de Padilla and Diego Lopez carried him tenderly to his

154

tiny quarters. The surgeon, the friar, and Captain Maldonado stayed constantly at his side, while the silent soldiers stood in little groups waiting for news.

They learned the cause of the accident: the new saddle girth had been stored so long that it had rotted.

All preparations for the eastern journey came to a standstill while Coronado's life hung in the balance.

Francisco opened his eyes upon a room whose walls seemed to spin around him. Faces and forms of men swam about dimly. He lowered his eyelids quickly. Sounds beat upon his ears as if from far away. But gradually it came to him that they were voices. He made out a few words: ". . . opened his eyes . . ." ". . . is alive . . ." "Will he live?"

He tried looking again. The swimming forms became still at last, and he knew Fray Juan, Don Rodrigo, Don Hernando . . .

"Of course I'll live," he grumbled at them. How haggard they all looked. "What's the matter with all of you?" he asked.

It was days later that he learned that they had grown haggard watching his long struggle with death. He had no memory of those weeks. Even now he had trouble with time. Sometimes he thought he was a boy in Spain. At other times he was in his big stone house in Mexico City. Then again he would find himself in Tiguex, in this pueblo called Alcanfor. It was confusing.

His recovery was slow, but at last the day came when he could put his feet to the floor and walk a step or two. One afternoon he walked all the way to the door. Ah, it was good to look out and see his comrades again. But what were those men doing in that little knot over there? Why did one duck out of sight? It was Captain Cardenas. But it couldn't be! Cardenas was on the way to Spain.

He let Fray Juan help him back to his cot. He put a hand to his aching head. "I must be losing my mind," he murmured. "I thought I saw Don Garcia."

He saw the friar exchange glances with Rodrigo Maldonado and Hernando de Alvarado. "We didn't mean for you to see him yet, until you are stronger," Father Padilla confessed.

Coronado's mind was suddenly clear. "Then he must have news you do not want me to hear."

The three men nodded. "The whole Sonora Valley is in revolt," Alvarado told him. "Captain Cardenas was not able to get through. He came back here to warn us."

"Let me talk with Don Garcia."

From Captain Cardenas, Coronado learned that Alcaraz, the villainous commander, had been killed by the avenging Opatas. The Spanish base had been abandoned. Some of the soldiers had fled south to Culiacan. Others, trapped north of the base, had met Cardenas and warned him not to enter the valley.

"No white man is safe there," Cardenas added. "Juan Gallego will never get through to you now with his supplies. We are cut off from New Spain."

"Don Garcia! Where is your courage?" the general thundered. "Not all the heathens in the New World can keep me from getting home! They can never cut us off from New Spain. We shall get through, never fear!"

The excitement sent Coronado into a relapse. The captains got him back to bed, but in his fever he kept muttering over and over his determination to return to Doña Beatrice and his children.

Their commander's homesickness released a flood of it in the Spaniards. They felt free now to express their own feelings. Some of them sent a petition to Coronado asking that the journey to Quivira be given up and they all go home. There were about sixty, however, who wanted to continue the search for treasure.

As soon as he was able to think about it, Francisco said the queston must be voted on by everyone in the expedition. "Of one thing I am certain," he said. "Whatever we do, we must do together."

The vote showed that the majority favored a return to New Spain.

Giving silent thanks, the general ordered plans made to leave for Mexico early in April, as soon as the snows melted. That would be a little more than two years since they had left Compostela that February day in 1540.

14

Coronado Comes Home

Francisco continued to live partly in a dream world. Often he thought Doña Beatrice was with him. Only now and then could he be sure that things around him were real and that he was actually hundreds of miles from his family.

On one such day, Fray Juan de Padilla sat in the chair beside him and spoke gently. "My son, I have a favor to ask. The missionaries wish to remain and minister to these pagan people. I myself wish to return and live with the Wichitas in Quivira."

Coronado put his head on his arms on the table and sat thus a long minute to be sure he had the words right in his head. "I have no authority over the Franciscans, Father," he said at last. "But you know what it means? You will probably never see New Spain again."

Fray Juan turned on him his warm, rueful, wise old smile. "And probably Heaven much sooner. Nevertheless, we have talked it over, and that is our wish."

"Then God be with you."

Some of the Spaniards thought the friars were crazy. "To live among these savages without arms!" Alvarado murmured, shaking his head.

"There is no weapon more powerful than the rosaries we carry," Father Padilla asserted firmly.

Coronado, seeing that they were determined, enjoyed helping with their preparations on the days when his head did not hurt too much. Fray Luis wished to stay in Pueblo country, with his headquarters at Pecos. He believed that the people of Bigotes could be converted into good Christians.

"They shall be my people," he told Coronado. He took to Pecos his chisel and adze for carving crosses, and a Negro boy as companion and servant. A little later the general sent some sheep to them. The soldiers who drove the flock to Pecos told the general, on their return, that they had met Fray Luis and the boy going to visit another town. They seemed to be in the good graces of

Pecos, except for the old medicine men. The friar suspected that the medicine men wanted to kill him.

Fray Juan de la Cruz wished to stay in Tiguex. To make things easier for him, the general released the Tiguas who had been slaves since the capture of Moho, telling them to rebuild their villages and live in peace.

That left the way clear for Father Padilla to return to Quivira. Coronado made a special effort to be up and cheerful the morning he was to leave. Spring was in the air, or at least the promise of it. The pack mules, carrying mostly church equipment, stood quietly except for the flicking of their long ears. Coronado stroked the shoulder of each animal.

He shook hands with the two Indian boys, Lucas and Sebastian, who had come with Fray Juan from his convent in Mexico and would not leave him now. They were herding a flock of sheep. Leading the only horse was a Portuguese gardener, Andres do Campo. "Take good care of our padre," Francisco said. "Serve him well."

When Fray Juan took his hand in both of his and blessed him, words failed Coronado. He could only press the rough hands and nod. His heart was heavy, as if parting forever from a beloved brother. As soon as the missionaries were out of sight, Alvarado had to help the general back to bed.

Nothing more was ever heard of Fray Luis or Fray Juan de la Cruz.

But about five years later, Andres do Campo, Lucas, and Sebastian turned up in Panuco, on the east coast of New Spain. Gaunt and sunbaked, they had walked from Quivira without compass or guide, living mostly on rabbits killed by two pet dogs which made the long journey with them. They had wandered southward from Kansas through Oklahoma and Texas, crossing the mountains near Monterrey, Mexico.

Do Campo explained that they were determined to reach New Spain alive in order to tell the world about the martyrdom of Fray Juan de Padilla.

Had their beloved padre been content to stay in Quivira, they believed, all would have gone well. But Fray Juan had wanted to visit a tribe to the east, to convert them. The Wichitas warned him that those people were of a very warlike nature, and were their enemies.

Fray Juan was not deterred, and of course Do Campo and the two boys went with him. A few days from Quivira, they saw Indians running toward them bedecked for war and shouting for the death of the missionary.

"Flee, my children," Father Padilla ordered. "Save yourselves, for me you cannot help."

162

He was on his knees with head uplifted in prayer when the arrows rained death upon him.

The Indians did not try to kill the others, but kept them in captivity. After ten months they were able to escape and start their amazing journey.

A few days after the friars had left Tiguex, the army was ready to start in the other direction.

No longer did their golden general ride at their head. He was carried on a cowhide litter swung on poles harnessed to two mules. To the man in the litter, days and nights ran together in a blur of pain. Only now and then did he know where he was and what was happening.

Hawikuh in Cibola he recognized, and some places on the craggy trail through the long wilderness brought back memories. At the Bad Pass he could tease some of the young soldiers who had flung their saddles on backward the night the Cibolanos had surprised them.

"We were so young then," they said now, two years and many events later.

Francisco crossed himself when they passed the Camp of Death where Espinosa had died from eating wild parsnips. How long ago that seemed!

He wakened once from a troubled sleep to find himself and his litter on a raft. They were crossing the Gila River.

He knew Red House when they reached it, its ancient caved-in walls as lonesome and mysterious as ever, but his mind became confused with the first time he had seen it. "Tell Melchior Diaz to find out how far it is to the sea," he murmured. How foolish he felt when Alvarado reminded him gently that Diaz was dead, killed on his own spear while looking for the sea and their ships.

Two days later, near the San Pedro River, Coronado's mules were halted. Maldonado and Alvarado sat beside their commander to shield him from the sun. He could hear a wild commotion of excited talk. He sat up. "What is happening?" he demanded.

"We have met Juan Gallego and his pack-train of supplies!"

No wonder there was excitement! Coronado rose. "How did he get through the Sonora Valley?" he asked quickly. "I must talk with him."

"We hurried, and we fought," the rugged old veteran explained to the general. "I came ahead with seven hard fighters, moving so fast that we took the Opata warriors by surprise, and slashing at them so fiercely that they thought we were not human. Fast as we went, the word of our coming went faster, and we began to find their villages deserted. For ten days we dashed through that valley without rest, giving them no time to organize themselves. The fifteen men following us with the baggage mules had a clear path. Not a Spaniard was killed, Your Grace."

"Excellent, Captain, excellent!" Francisco told him. "Then you can take us back through the valley in the same way."

Gallego dropped his eyes. The tough men of his little band, standing behind him, shifted on their feet uneasily. After a minute, Gallego looked up and said, "We had expected to continue to the new lands. Now that you have our supplies, will you not go back north?"

Francisco wanted to say no, finally and flatly. Instead, he asked Diego Lopez to find out what the majority of the men wanted to do. In a few hours Captain Lopez reported back. "Those who opposed our leaving Tiguex in the first place wish to turn around. But the greater number want to go home."

"So be it," Gallego agreed, in spite of his disappointment.

"Good soldier! Show us the way," Coronado murmured, and went back to his litter.

The Opatas in the long narrow valley of the Sonora River were still scattered. They remembered the fury of

Gallego too well to attack the Spaniards openly. But they made the nights hideous with their yells. They killed some of the horses.

Traveling as fast as they could, the Spaniards left the warriors behind them and came to the villages of the still-friendly Pimas around Corazones. They hurried on across the Mayo River and the Fuerte. On the banks of the Sinaloa they took time to rest and enjoy the melons and beans given them by the peaceful natives of the straw huts.

It would not be far, then, to Culiacan, that outpost of the province of New Galicia, of which Coronado was still governor.

One night Rodrigo Maldonado sat spraddle-legged on the grassy floor of the general's tent, honing the fine Toledo blade of his knife to razor sharpness. Coronado watched him lazily, letting his eyes wander from his dark friend to the darker shadow of him set dancing on the tent wall by flickering torches. He was feeling a little better now that they were through the Opata country and the traveling was easier. The most cheering thought was that this was their last camp before entering Culiacan. He admitted to himself that he was looking forward to good beds and food cooked in kitchens.

The men who lived in Culiacan were riding on

through the night. They would take word of the army's approach. All over camp the soldiers were cleaning themselves up and brushing their horses to be ready for their welcome home to New Spain.

Francisco, too, wanted to be at his best. He picked up his silver mirror, looked at himself, and grimaced. He wondered if even Doña Beatrice would recognize the pale, hollow-eyed, wind-blown wretch who grimaced back at him. He ran his fingers through his long brown hair and the matted beard which jutted out below his bony cheeks.

Captain Maldonado tested the knife on one edge of his own thick beard. "There, now!" he muttered with satisfaction. "Don Francisco, the best barber in this army is at your service."

"Trim Don Garcia first," Francisco replied, nodding toward Captain Cardenas, who had been looking on in gloomy silence.

Maldonado grinned and moved a torch closer to the captain.

Cardenas told him wryly, "Even the best barber in the king's court could not give us the look of heroes, Don Rodrigo. Not with our rusty corselets and tattered clothes."

Francisco's eyes flashed briefly with his old fire.

"Nevertheless, friend Garcia, we shall hold our heads high, as heroes might."

Maldonado beamed. "Ay, Don Francisco, that is the way to feel! We have been good soldiers and good Spaniards. Who is to say, then, that we are not heroes?"

"The king, most likely," Cardenas grumbled, "in that we return empty-handed."

Coronado said nothing. He knew that the burning of the warriors at Arenal still lay heavy on the mind and heart of Captain Cardenas. Well, it was enough to make a man gloomy, that and a useless right arm.

Next morning the general was helped into the saddle of his beloved and faithful chestnut stallion, so that he could once again ride at the head of his force. Maldonado and Alvarado rode on each side, alert to steady him should he become dizzy.

About midday they were met by the officials of Culiacan, who had ridden forth to greet them. "Because of your injury, Your Grace," the mayor said, "we have planned no noisy welcome. But our people are happy to have you back. We hope you will rest here a long time."

The general was taken to the best house in town. He accepted gratefully the new, clean clothes ready for him. Even more gratefully he gave himself to the soft bed. The ride had taken all his strength.

But the next day was a busy one. Many people came to see him. He talked longest with the two captains, Diego Lopez and Pedro de Tovar. They wished to stay in Culiacan, to make it their home.

"Are there others who wish to live here?"

"Yes," they replied, "a goodly number."

So Coronado issued orders that anyone was free to drop out of the expedition whenever he wished. One who remained in Culiacan was Pedro de Castañeda, a plain soldier who, twenty years later, wrote the fullest account of the journey.

When Coronado left Culiacan, it was with a much smaller force. This worried Captain Cardenas, who said, "We shall not make a good showing in Mexico City."

Francisco murmured weakly, "What difference does it make, Don Garcia? I would not have weary men journey farther only for that. In truth, it is my hope to slip into the city with as little notice as possible."

This time Coronado did not try to ride, but was willing to be carried on his litter, all the way to Compostela. Here in his little capital he rested a week, learning how the province had fared in his absence and talking with old friends. One of them gave him a gentle dappled-gray mare with a smooth gait.

When they reached the new and bustling little city

of Guadalajara, Coronado was told some gossip. The viceroy, it was being whispered, was so displeased with the outcome of the expedition that he would refuse to see the captain-general. Some were saying that all the officers were to be brought to trial for misspending money and for injustice to the Indians.

Coronado's anger rose. "Tell me no more!" he thundered. It was enough to take the heart out of the strongest of men. It made his head hurt worse than it ever had. As they drew closer and closer to home, Coronado stayed to himself, not wanting to talk to anyone. Questions went round and round in his mind, tormenting him. Would everyone blame him for not finding gold?

And then there was the worst thought of all, the one he could barely bring himself to face: if the viceroy had turned against him, what would Madame Estrada, his mother-in-law, who had put much money into the expedition, do? And what of Doña Beatrice herself? How would she receive a husband broken in health, bereft of fortune, in disgrace before the world?

The general turned his army over to Captain Tristan de Arellano. Up and up they climbed into the green, forested mountains. From some of the turns in the trail hundreds of rugged peaks could be seen at once. But Francisco scarcely noticed. Then one day they topped

170

the last pass and could look into the valley where lay the lovely island city that was home.

Now at last Francisco tried to gather himself together. He called for the gentle dappled mare, determined to ride the rest of the way. Once more he took command. He had sent Doña Beatrice a letter from Guadalajara, telling her that he was on the way home. But he refused now to let messengers go ahead to tell the time of their arrival.

So there was no fanfare — no one at all to greet them — as the tired little group clattered over the stone causeway. One by one the men dropped out to go to their homes, with brief good-bys. Only a handful were with Francisco when he rode past the church of Santo Domingo, where he had been married, past the palace of Cortéz, past the cathedral, round the Plaza, and over the canal to his own house. They rode on to the back, to the carriage entrance.

By that time they had been seen. There was a growing hubbub of voices and running feet as servants rushed to swing back the gates. Before Francisco could be helped from his mount, he saw Doña Beatrice flying across the patio to fall into his arms. Tears of relief and joy streamed down her face.

Then there were the two little girls to be hugged.

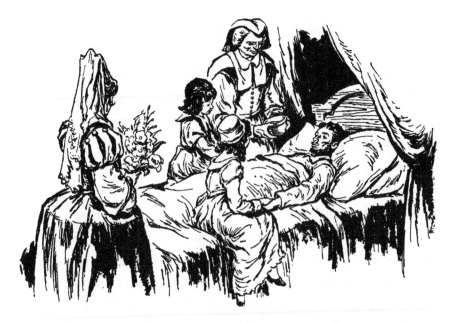

And there was Madame Estrada to embrace him warmly and order him carried to his room, which was filled with flowers.

Francisco was limp with happiness. He was at home! And he was loved and welcomed! Nothing was changed in the big stone house except that Isabel and Marina had grown so big in two and a half years. They were shy at first, but soon they were sitting on his bed, holding his hand, bringing all their favorite toys to show him.

Madame Estrada busied herself seeing to his comfort. Doña Beatrice would not leave his bedside. When he sought to apologize for their lost fortune, she hushed him. "What matter about that? You have come home. And the Franciscans may do wonders in that far land. Some day settlers may go there, following your trail, to build good homes and to make all that land truly Spanish. Let us be happy about that."

Only the meeting with the viceroy worried Francisco now. His wife sought to ease his mind on that, too. "He has given no hint of displeasure to me," she assured him. "I think it is just talk."

Francisco smiled at her. How good she was! No wonder the poor and needy were calling her "the saint." He told her, "I shall call on him in the morning, and then we shall know."

But next morning, while Francisco was having his breakfast of melon and chocolate under the bougainvillea vine in the patio, the viceroy came to see him. In only a minute Francisco's worries were over, for Mendoza's smile and embrace were as warm as ever.

Coronado told him of the gossip. "Why do they say those things?" he demanded.

Mendoza's black eyes snapped under an angry frown. "The complaints and mutterings, Don Francisco, come from some who put their money, but not themselves, into this gamble. Now they would tear you down to save their own pride. They have tried to turn me against you, but they have not succeeded. Nor shall they!"

Never had Francisco heard more comforting words. Before he could answer, the viceroy went on, "Let them say the expedition is a failure. It is true we had hoped for treasure, and not finding it is a disappointment. But think of the knowledge you have brought back to us! The map-makers will be busy for a long time catching up with you. And who knows what may yet happen in those new lands whose door you have opened?"

Francisco chewed on a honey-cake, looking thoughtfully across the table at the viceroy, who went on, "Furthermore, I say this was the best led of any expedition in the New World. Less than twenty of our men dead after all that traveling! And less than thirty dead of our Indian allies. What other commander has such a record?"

"After those words," Francisco replied with a smile, "it matters not what anyone else thinks." Then he raised his eyebrows and asked, "Am I to be replaced as governor of New Galicia?"

"Do you want to be?" Mendoza asked in return.

"No. There are things that need doing in the province, and I should like to do them."

Mendoza threw back his head and laughed in the way Francisco remembered so well. "I was just thinking," he explained, "how different you sound from that day I named you governor. The place is yours, my son, for as long as you want it."

Winter is a mild season in Guadalajara. The sun lends warmth to stone and adobe walls. The Pacific breeze is never harsh. During the winter of 1543, Coronado, who had made Guadalajara the capital of New Galicia in place of Compostela, enjoyed living there with Doña Beatrice and their children. He had schools, churches, and roads built. Under his rule the village began the growth which would one day make it Mexico's second largest city.

Because his head injury still troubled him, Coronado asked to be relieved of the governorship. The rest of his life was spent quietly in his beloved Mexico City, where he served again on the council and twice was procurator mayor. Coronado never wholly recovered his health, and he lived only fourteen years from that February morning in 1540 when he set out on his great adventure.

Though he had courage to spare, both in facing unknown dangers and in standing up for what he believed to be right, Coronado had little of the aggressive spirit of the first *conquistadores*. Warmhearted and loyal, but not overly ambitious, he was satisfied with knowing that he had performed his duty to the best of his ability.

Coronado did not think of himself as a hero, nor did many of the people of his time. He found no gold or other treasure, and the great and enduring results of his discoveries could not be foreseen. He left his name and his memory over all of northern Mexico and the sprawling Southwest of the United States to become a permanent link between two great republics. Later, both Spanish and English settlers would find their own riches in the regions Coronado had discovered.

As long as the Republic of Mexico and the United States endure, the name of Francisco Vasquez de Coronado will be a mutual source of pride joining them in friendliness. For Coronado is a true hero for both countries: daring, competent, loyal, and humane.